Coding With

PYTHON

Python Tips and Tricks
to Write Better Codes

ALEXANDER CANE

Table of Contents

Introduction

Python is a multipurpose dynamic programming language. The main principle of the Python is code readability and its simple syntax, which allows programmers to write the code quickly and efficiently.

Python supports multiple programming paradigms scaling from object-oriented to functional programming. Like Perl's CPAN, Python has comprehensive standard libraries. Python can be used for system programming (many components of Linux distribution are programmed in Python) as well as for application programming. In the field of Web Programming, Python has proved its existence. Django, Pylons, Turbogear and Web2py are some of web framework which runs on Python. You can write a full-fledged game in Python.

Main Features of Python

Let us see some of the main features of Python, which makes it a powerful programming language to write simple, efficient and better codes.

1. Very easy to understand and reliable: Python uses a straightforward programming syntax so that the programmers can learn it quickly, and it is easy for them to write the codes. It also makes the code maintainable and reusable for future changes in the application in case the original programmer who has written the code is no longer available. Thus, the new programmer can easily edit or reuse the same piece of code written in Python without facing any handover related problems. This makes Python reliable for writing better codes.

2. Cross-platform support and portable: Python is a powerful programming language that can run on most of the Operating systems like Windows, Linux, UNIX, and Mac OS. The code can be run on any machine and no need to worry about the system resources required for running the code on a different machine other than which it was written on. Thus, it makes Python portable.

3. Open source and free to use: Python has been designed to be freely modified as well as re-distributed under the OSI approved source license. It can be used for commercial use as well. Thus, it is entirely free to use, and

programmers/organizations need not pay any license fees to write codes in Python programming language. Python's community support is having a large user base of open source developers.

4. Object-Oriented programming language: Python support all the OOP concepts like classes, objects, encapsulation, inheritance, and polymorphism. It is also called as DRY (Don't Repeat Yourself). The main focus of Python programming language is to create reusable code so that the existing code can be used in the future as well with little tweaks.

5. Use of whitespaces: Most of the programming languages use the curly braces to begin/end the blocks. They are called as opening and closing parenthesis. Python has made it easier by using the significant whitespaces instead. Thus, the indentation of the whitespaces determines which code groups are written together.

6. Memory management: All the memory allocation related tasks, including the dynamic memory allocation, is handled by Python's inbuilt memory manager. This makes it easy for the programmers to focus only on the coding part and write better codes instead of getting worried about the memory allocation tasks. This is very important when programmers want to optimize their code so that it runs much faster than it is now.

7. Exceptions: Python provides an extensive range of exceptions, which covers all the crucial issues which might come up in your code while compiling or running it. Thus, by using these exception handling, programmers can write cleaner codes that do not end up in getting hanged or not responding.

8. Extensive standard library: Python's standard library is very powerful and provides all modern features for writing better codes like File Input/Output mechanism, text processing mechanism, web programming, data compression, multithreading, cryptographic authentications, networking, internet protocols, development tools, debugging, runtime services, custom interpreters, and more. Therefore, Python standardized solutions to deal with the common issues in programming.

Now let us see some of the misconceptions related to Python programming among the programmers and developers.

The Misconception

There is a general misconception in the programming community that Python performance is slower than most of the competent programming languages like Java, C, and C++. When we choose a particular programming language, we not only look into the execution speed but also look into other aspects like style of coding (mainly about the syntax and semantics), time to develop the code, availability of standard library, implementations, etc. One cannot compare the programming language based only on its execution speed.

Having some of the excellent features like rapid development, high scalability, powerful standard library, cross-platform portability, Python programming language is one of the popular choices in the programming community.

Basic Tips and Tricks in Python

In this chapter, we are going to share few tips and tricks for all the Python coders and programmers so that they can write better codes. It will also help them in making their already written coding simple to understand, optimized, and reusable.

Only a few programmers know that a large size code can be reduced considerably by implementing many tips and tricks in Python programming. This not only helps in making the code efficient but also reduces the time taken by the code for its execution. Thus, the code becomes faster than it was before.

Now let us see some of the basic tricks.

Checking if a String Contains a Substring without Find()

You probably know that you can test if a list, tuple, or dictionary contains an item by testing the expression 'item in list' or 'item not in the list.' The same concept works for a string also in Python.

The traditional and old way to find a part of a string in the main string is:

```
>>> # main string will be like this:
>>> string = "Hello world example"
>>> # we are finding the string "world."
>>> if string.find("world") != -1 :
...     print "String is found."

Output: String is found
```

Now let us see the trick to search it in a faster ad efficient way.

```
>>> # main string will be like this:
>>> string = "Hello world example"
>>> # we are finding the string "world."
>>> if "world" in the string:
... print "String is found."
...
Output: String is found
```

Therefore, by using the above trick, there is no need for the programmer to remember what will be returned by the find() method.

Printing List, the Customized Approach

Printing the data present in a list is never easy, but a simple solution to it is **using the "join" method in the string.**

```
>>> # let us take a list which has three strings present in it.
>>> valuesList = [ "Value1", "Value2", Value3]
```

```
>>> print "The 3 latest values are: %s"
%","".join(valuesList)
>>> The 3 latest values are: Value1,Value2,Value3
```

Here, by using the join method, we are tuning the list to a string. Each item present in the list is cast as a string and then connected with a string to call on. We are using the delimiter.

This method is faster as it is running in the best possible linear time. It is not using the sequence unpacking method, which is generally slower.

Division of Integer and Float Values

Dividing an integer by another integer will result in the truncation of the value to an integer only. For e.g., If we divided seven by two, then we will get the result as three.

To fix this thing, there are two methods.

First method is to use one float and one integer value. It is straightforward to make an integer value into float value by appending a decimal 0 after the number, like 7.0, and this will automatically return the result of 7.0/2 as 3.5, which solves our problem.

If you don't want to use the first method, there is another method with neat and clean code. There is an inbuilt directory for Python from_future_import division. This will always give the output as a float value whenever any division takes place in the Python code. Once you have imported it, the result of 7/2 will be 3.5 only.

In case you still need the truncated value somewhere in your code, then you can always use the / / operator, which will truncate the decimal value automatically, and the result of 7/2 will be 3.

Both the methods are very useful whenever you need to truncate the decimal parts or want to keep the decimal part after the division of 2 numbers.

Constructing Dictionaries with Keyword Arguments – Refined Approach

Any keyword arguments you pass to the dict constructor are added to the newly created dictionary before returning.

For example:

```
>>> dict (a = 1, b = 2)
{'a' : 1, 'b': 2}
```

This will make your code much cleaner than creating a regular dictionary. It depends upon your written code. When you use this, there will be fewer quotes in your code, and this makes it look simple.

Converting List to Dictionary - Simple Approach

A python list of list with two elements in it can be directly converted into a python dictionary.

For example:

```
>>> dict_list = [ [ 'x', 1], ['y', 2], ['z', 3] ]
>>> dictionary = dict {dict_list)
>>> print dictionary
{'x' : 1, 'y' : 2, 'z' : 3}
```

This is a simple way to create a dictionary from the format of the list as explained above.

Converting all the Data Types into Strings – using Inbuilt Functions

Sometimes there is a need to store the data **structures in some file for later use**, so the data present in list or dictionary can be directly converted into a string which can be easily written into the file **using "repr()" and "eval()" methods**.

```
>>> list1 = [1, [2, 3], 4]
>>> print list1
[1, [2, 3], 4]
>>> # We will use the repr() method to convert the complete
list to a string
>>> list1_new = repr (list1)
>>> list1_new
'[1, [2, 3], 4]'
>>> Now to convert in back we can use the eval() method
>>> eval(list1_new)
```

The same thing also works with dictionary.

This is helpful when **there is a need to store the complete data of** a data structure in some text file for reference.

Accessing Type with Python – When Type is Unknown

Sometimes when there are different types of data present in one data structure, and we are not sure on type of data is present, we can use "isinstance()" method to compare various types in Python.

isinstance() method takes two arguments, variable to be tested and the type (int, list, dict, etc).

This is mostly useful in cases where we are **not sure of the value type present** in that data structure.

Python Type Checking

Earlier, types were defined and handled by Python's in-built interpreter in an implicit manner. But now, as Python has evolved in recent years, the latest versions of Python allow the developers to specify the explicit type hints, which can then be used by many tools to make your code more efficient and modular.

Type systems are present in every programming language, including Python, to categorize the objects under which category they fall. For example, a type system can have a number value like 95 which is an example of the numerical type object. Similarly, a string type will have a set of characters in it, like the name of a person, country, place, meaningful data, etc.

Dynamic Typing

In dynamic programming, Python's interpreter checks the data type only once the code starts running. It is not checked while the code is getting compiled. This make the type of the variable to change between its lifespan.

Let us see the below example, which shows that Python uses dynamic typing.

```
>>> if False:
...      2 + "three" # this line is not going to run ever;
therefore it will not show the TypeError being raised
... else:
...      2 + 3
...
5

>>> 2 + "three" # now it will get for type checking, and
then it will show a TypeError being raised
TypeError: unsupported operand type(s) for +: 'str' and
'int'
```

Therefore, we can say that the TypeError did not come in the first line because it never ran and no chance of getting it type-checked. But in the second case, as soon as the 2 + "three" line got run, it checked for the TypeError and then showed the error because we cannot add a string value and an integer value together in Python.

Now we will see if the variables present in Python code can change its type.

```
>>> value = "My program"
>>> type(value)
<class 'str'>
>>> value = 50.6
>>> type(value)
<class 'float'>
```

In the above code, the type() method provide the object type. By seeing the above values in the returned by type() method, we can say that type changing is allowed in Python, and the latest value is used in Python. Initially, the object type of Python of value for Python was "String," but then it was changed to "Float" later.

Type checking provides a little documentation to your code. You can also use type hints to catch certain types of errors in your Python code. Earlier, developers were using docstring to document the expected types present inside a method's arguments. But it lacked the automatic checks as docstrings have no fixed standards.

Type hints also help in improving the linters and Integrated Development Environments (IDEs). They help in providing static reasons of what your code is doing. This makes them offer better predictions and code completion. The only thing you need to keep in mind as a developer is that type hints will take time and effort both for adding to your Python code.

Guide To Write more Readable Python Code

Why Does Readability Matter?

Python is often described as being more than merely a coding language and more of a philosophy of a language.

Conceived in the late '80s, Python mainly had two tenets –

1. Make a developer's code more readable.

2. Reduce the lines of code while achieving the same effect in terms of efficiency and functionality.

Although using whitespace as indent and doing away with curly braces (except for dictionaries) has dramatically enhanced the readability feature of python, there's much more than one can do to make a developing code much more readable.

So one may ask, how does it help?

The development community widely accepts that over 70% of the actual effort and total capital is spent on maintenance. It's highly probable that the developer will not be maintaining the code that he wrote, and instead, the work would be done by another person who'll have to read through somebody else's code. Having an easy to read code in such scenarios help the maintenance process be efficient.

It saves the client a lot of capital and reduces stress for the maintenance team as well.

We can now have a look at how we can increase readability further and make our python code more readable, easily maintainable and developer-friendly.

Limit your Lines

This is a golden rule that should be followed across the code. For general code like method declaration and inline method calls etc. limit your line to a maximum of **79 characters**.

For comments and "docstrings," it is recommended to use a **72 character** limit per line.

This is recommended keeping in mind that there still are devices that have a default wrapping at 80 characters and in case your code line exceeds that length the line get broken up at awkward locations, making the code very ugly and at time unreadable.

To break long lines into smaller ones, wrap the whole statement in a set of parentheses, preferably and break and indent your line conveniently.

You can also break your line by adding a "\," i.e., a backslash at the intended end of your physical line and continue your logical line, but it is not a recommended practice as it makes the code difficult to read.

Use Proper Indents

Unless you have an old code that still uses eight white spaces for a tab, you should use four white spaces for a tab or put just four spaces. The number of white spaces per tab is usually configurable in a few platforms like Eclipse.

Apart from using python's inbuilt line joining logic for codes present inside parentheses, we can also use "hanging indents" for continuing lines for the parameter list where the next line is aligned to the opening delimiter.

If you are not aligning the next line to the opening delimiter, to make the code distinguishable, we should keep in mind that the first line should not have any arguments, and we must add indents till we reach some clarity.

Blank Lines

The thumb rule for inserting blank lines is as follows:

1. Use two blank lines to separate Top-level methods and class definitions.

2. Child methods definitions of a class should have a single blank line.

3. Sparingly use blank lines to separate a cluster of similar functions.

4. Use blank lines in functions to highlight logical sections but sparingly.

Imports

We should put modular imports in different lines, but if you are importing multiple contents from a single module, we can put it in a single line in itself.

When you are grouping imports, it should be in the below order:
1. Importing standard library
2. Importing third party related imports.
3. Importing the local library or application related imports.

Don't:

```
>>> from module import *
```

This is a bad practice and should always be avoided.

Comments

There are two methods of writing non-logical statements in python-

1. Using hash character, E.g.: "#."
2. Using triple quotes, E.g. ''' ''' or """ """

These two are made for particular purposes, and we should use them only in the context they are supposed to be used.

We use the hash character to start Block Comments and Inline Comments and triple quotes to enclose Document Strings only!

Block Comments

These comments apply to some of the code that follows or in some cases, all of the code that follows.

Each line of the comment segment starts with "#" and followed by white space. Paragraphs inside a comment block are separated by a line containing a single "#."

Inline Comments

Comments on the same line as the logical statement are best avoided unless necessary and if they are stating more than the obvious.

Document Strings

A document string, ideally, should be present as the first line(s) in every module, function, class, or method. This *docstring* will become the value for the __doc__ attribute for that module. This not only makes it easier to understand the purpose of a module/method etc. but also helps you to auto-create help documents for an entire application easily.

Naming Conventions

Which names not to be used

Refrain from using lowercase letter "el" (l), uppercase letter "oh" (O), or uppercase letter "eye" (I) as variable names. These characters are, in some fonts, indistinguishable from the numerals (1) one and (0) zero.

Class Names

Class names should follow the *CamelCase* convention. If there are private classes meant only for the internal use, we should append an underscore as shown below:

```
>>>class _InternalClass(object)
```

Exception Names

In Python, exceptions are classes as well, so the naming convention explained above for classes applies here. But you can use the suffix "Error" in the exception names list if they are not actually "Errors."

Function Names

Functions and methods should usually have lowercase words, which are having underscores to separate them and to ease the code reading/glancing process. We can use *pascalCase* if it is already being used in the code to conform to the prevailing style.

Method Arguments

You need to use self as the first argument always to instantiate the methods. Similarly, you need to use cls as the first argument in the case of class methods present in the code.

Method Names

For methods, as mentioned before, use lowercase words and separate them using underscores. It is required to make the code more readable.

All the nonpublic methods, as well as the instance variables, should begin with an underscore; this is the only way to distinguish private from public attributes or methods.

Constants

Use All Caps for constants and separate words with underscores and define them on a modular level. E.g., SUM_COUNT and TOTAL_DEFICIT.

Performance Tuning Tips

Introduction

This chapter contains a collection of some tips and tricks that helps to improve the performance of the code written in Python language by the programmers. We have collected some of the best coding practices used by the programmer's community and tried to present it with the help of sample code along with proof of its performance.

Now let us see some of the performance tuning tips.

List Comprehension

List comprehension is a beautiful concept in python, which is taken from LISP. Using the list comprehension, we can generate a list simply and elegantly. If you are doing any calculation and the result is list, then it is advisable to use list comprehension instead of loop. To give a simple example- I need to find out a square of list numbers and assign it to a list.

Below examples shows the way to generate the list using Looping method and using list comprehension method. Please note that the list comprehension code looks decent, and it takes less time to execute.

```
import timeit
# List generation using Loop
def withLoop():
    natual_squares = []
    for i in range(100):
        natual_squares.append(i * i)
    return natual_squares


# List generation using list comprehension method
def withLC():
    natual_squares = [i * i for i in range(100)]
    return natual_squares


# execution time calculations
with_loop =  timeit.timeit("withLoop()", setup = "from
__main__ import withLoop",number = 1)
with_LC = timeit.timeit("withLC()", setup = "from __main__
import withLC", number = 1)
print "List Comprehension Method :%f \nWith Loop Method
%f" % (with_LC, with_loop)
```

Now let us see the output of the above program.

```
C:\windows\system32\cmd.exe

List Comprehension Method :0.000024
With Loop Method 0.000031
```

Therefore, we can see that the execution time for the Comprehension method is 0.000024, which is less than the time taken by the Loop method (0.000031). Hence, the code is executing at a faster rate when we are using the Comprehension method trick in Python programming.

Python Strings

Usage of long strings in Python programming can affect the performance of the Python code. Python considers the string as mutable objects. This means each time the string is assigned to a variable, a new object is created in the memory. The most obvious method used by the programmer during string programming is the use of concatenations, which is the use of += operator to join the string. Since Python considers string as mutable, each time a string is assigned to a variable a new object is created in the memory and assigns the new value. So using a loop to construct a long string out of small strings is not an efficient way in Python.

If you are dealing with the concatenation of long string by joining the small string, it is advisable to use '.join' operator instead of using '+=' operator. The join method is faster and cleaner compared to the conventional '+=' operator method. This can be illustrated by giving a simple example.

```
import timeit
# List contains the English alphabets
wordList = ['A', 'B', 'C', 'D', 'E', 'F', 'G', 'H']
```

```
# Function uses the normal string concatenation method.
def concateUsingAssign(words):
    wordString = ""
    for i in words:
        wordString += i
    return wordString


# Function uses .join() operator for the concatenation.
def concateUsingJoin(words):
    return ','.join(words)


# execution time calcuations
with_concateUsingAssign =
timeit.timeit("concateUsingAssign(wordList)", setup =
"from __main__ import concateUsingAssign, wordList",
number = 1)
with_concateUsingJoin =
timeit.timeit("concateUsingJoin(wordList)", setup = "from
__main__ import concateUsingJoin, wordList", number = 1)
print "Concatenation using '+=' operator :%f
\nConcatenation using '.join()' operator %f"
%(with_concateUsingAssign, with_concateUsingJoin)
```

Now let us see the output of the above program.

24

In the above program, we take a small example of concatenating a string from the list. The first method 'concateUsingAssign()' uses the normal string concatenation and the second method 'concateUsingJoin()' uses the '.join' operation.

In the second method, we don't have to loop through the list. The '.join' operator does that for us. Therefore, we can clearly see that the time taken by the second method is less than the time taken by the first method for the code execution. This clearly indicates that the second master is faster.

Slice Operation on List

Another feature of the list in Python is the list slice. The list slice is performed by specifying two indices, namely 'start slice index' and 'end slice index.' The return value is a new list containing all the elements of the list, in order starting with the start slice index up to (but not including) end slice index.

A slicing syntax also supports an optional third argument called the 'Step" The step specifies the incremental step. The syntax of the List Slice is shown in below section.

```
Syntax
New_List = Current_List [start index : end index : step ]
```

Normally List Slicing operations are faster than the using conventional loops. We will see this with a program. The program generates odd numbers from the list of natural numbers.

```
import timeit
# Defined the list of values
natural_numbers = range(10000)
# Generation of odd natural numbers using loop
def genOddWithLoop(natnum):
    odd_num
    for i in natnum:
        if i % 2 <> 0 :
            odd_num.append(x)
    return odd_num


# Generation of odd natural numbers using list slice
functionality
def genOddWithSlice(natnum):
    return natnum[1:len(natnum):2]
# execution time calcuations
with_loop = timeit.timeit("genOddWithLoop", setup = "from
__main__ import genOddWithLoop, natural_numbers", number =
1)
with_list_slice =  timeit.timeit("genOddWithSlice", setup
= "from __main__ import genOddWithSlice, natural_numbers",
number = 1)
print "Odd number Generation (Loop method) :%.10f \nOdd
number Generation (Slice method) %.10f"
%(with_loop,with_list_slice)
```

Now let us see the output of the above program.

```
C:\windows\system3Z\cmd.exe
Odd number Generation (Loop method) :0.0000007604
Odd number Generation (Slice method) 0.0000003802
```

As we can see that the Slice method took half the time taken by Loop method for the code execution. Therefore, it is clearly visible that the List slice method will execute faster than the conventional loops. This can even be optimized with the use of List compression.

Membership Search is Faster in Set and Dictionaries than List

Membership search in sets are faster than the list. This is because the list in python is implemented using dynamic array, and the Sets are implemented using hash tables. This implementation of these data structures gives them different characteristics. For instance, the hash table has a very fast lookup time, but cannot store the order of insertions. Please note that sets can be very fast when we need to find out if the object is available in a set, but at the same time, it becomes slower while iterating the elements in the set. See the below program. The program will search a random number from the huge list and set. In this example, the set works faster than the list.

```
import timeit
# Defined the list of values
lst = range(1,10000)
st = set(range(1,10000))
ele = 2698
```

```
# Function to search an element from list
def findInList(lst, ele):
    if ele in lst:
        return ele
    else:
        return None
# Function to search an element from Set
def findInSet(st, ele):
    if ele in st:
        return ele
    else:
        return None

# execution time calcuations
with_lst = timeit.timeit("findInList", setup = "from
__main__ import findInList, lst, st, ele", number = 1)
with_st = timeit.timeit("findInSet", setup = "from
__main__ import findInSet, lst, st, ele", number = 1)
print "Search in List :%.10f \nSearch in Set %.10f"
%(with_lst,with_st)
if with_lst > with_st:
    print "Search in Set is faster"
else:
    print "Search in List is faster"
```

Now let us see the output of the above program.

28

As we can see that the Search in List took double the time taken by Search in Set for the code execution. Therefore, it is clearly visible that the Search in Set will execute faster than the Search in Lists.

Avoid Printing to STDOUT

Normally programmer used to print the results to the STDOUT to check the control of the flow. If you are using the print statement in between your source code for debugging or checking the control flow of the code, it will affect the execution speed of the code. This is because whenever you use the print statement in the code, the arguments which are passed to the print statement need to be converted into a string before sending it to the console. This is a costly operation. Use of print statements in the Python web frameworks, like Django and Pylons, will reduce the performance of the web application. It is a good idea to discard all the print statements before moving the code to the production environment.

Instead of using the print statement, Python provides a wonderful library called logging. Using this library, you can avoid the print statement and redirect the printing statements to the log file. You can also use this logging feature for debugging and checking the control statements.

Profilers and Python Code

A profiler is a Python library which will help the programmer to analyze the different aspect of source code optimization. Profiling provides detailed information on all the functions and methods in a python source code. It also indicates the execution time spent on each method and functions. The most common profiler library is 'cProfile' and 'profile.' The profile library is purely a Python module and adds much overhead for the profiled programs. Therefore, the main focus should be on cProfile.

Profilers will help the programmer to analyze the Python source code. Using profilers, we can determine how much memory the program uses, is there any memory leak is happening, if there is any memory leak is happening, it also locates the exact location of the code where the memory leak is happening. There are some profilers available which will measure and report line-by-line timing and execution information to the programmers.

Code Profiling will help you to find the bottlenecks present in the Python code. This will provide the best possible information about the particular part of your code, which is taking the longest time to run. We can use this information to our rescue by looking at the information and taking appropriate steps to optimize that part. This will make your program more efficient than before.

Calculate Execution Time

Sometimes it is very important to know the execution time of the individual function calls or code statements, especially when you are working on a large scale application that has a large amount of data and processing involved in it. It comes handy as you will get to know which functions defined by you are taking a lot of execution time in a process. To help you with this, IPython provides you with the in-built commands to check your code's execution time easily.

You won't like to use the in-built time module to check your execution time as it is very repetitive and tedious task. Its function time.clock() is not used much now because of the same reason.

IPython has two in-built functions to automate the above problem for you. They are %time and %timeit.

%time will check the statement one at a time by running it and then gives you the total execution time. For example, you have a relatively huge list of strings, and you want to know the performance timing of different methods to select the strings which start with a prefix specified by you.

Here is a list of 5,00,000 strings and two similar methods to perform the above logic for the strings starting with the prefix 'book'.

```
# Huge list of 5 lakh strings
```

```
allStrings = [ 'book', 'notebook', 'pen', 'school',
'teacher' ] * 100000
firstMethod = [ i for i in strings if i.startswith('book') ]
secondMethod = [ i for i in strings if i[:4] == 'book']
```

You will think that both will have the same execution time. We can check it using the %time command:

```
In [ 243 ]: %time firstMethod = [ i for i in strings if
i.startswith('book') ]
CPU times: user 0.15 s, sys: 0.00 s, total: 0.15 s
Wall time: 0.15 s
In [ 244 ]: %time secondMethod = [ i for i in strings if
i[:4] == 'book' ]
CPU times: user 0.07 s, sys: 0.00 s, total: 0.07 s
Wall time: 0.07 s
```

Here the Wall time is the main thing to be considered. Therefore, as per the above wall time, we can see that the firstMethod took double time than the secondMethod. But it is not actually the precise timing. You can check it yourself by rerunning the above codes, and again, you will notice that the results are not always the same. Therefore, to have precise and accurate timing, we need to use the %timeit command. When we provide any random statement to %timeit, it will run the statement multiple times to provide a fairly precise execution time.

```
In [ 245 ]: %timeit [ i for i in strings if
i.startswith('book') ]
Ten loops, best of 2: 068 ms per loop
In [ 246 ]: %timeit [ i for i in strings if i[:4] == 'book'
]
```

```
Ten loops, best of 2: 641 ms per loop
```

This example illustrates the importance of Python's standard library functions to check your code's performance. Libraries like pandas and NumPy are really helpful in performance management in the large scale applications where every millisecond matters.

%timeit comes very handy when you want to analyze the functions and statements, having very little execution time. It can give you detailed results from microseconds to nanoseconds. When you have any function which gets called a million times, these time will microseconds will add up together to have a difference of seconds or even minutes in your overall data analysis timing. Let's see the below example:

```
In [ 247 ]: a = 'book'
In [ 248 ]: b = 'books'
In [ 249 ]: %timeit a.startswith(b)
1000000 loops, best of 2: 893 ns per loop
In [ 250 ]: %timeit a[:4] == b
10000000 loops, best of 2: 784 ns per loop
```

Using Timers

With the help of timers, we can find out the execution time of any part in the program. They can be put anywhere in the program. It provide the exact time and helps in improving the code where it is taking too long to execute.

Let us see some examples:

```
# first thing is to import the "time" module
import time
startTime = time.time()
print("Time aken")
print("% s sec" % (time.time() - startTime))
```

Output:

```
Time taken
0.01718357168148451 sec
```

Another example:

```
# first thing is to import the "time" module
import time
def xyz():
        startTime = time.time()
        print("Time taken")
        endTime = time.time()
        print(" xyz() method takes", endTime-startTime,
"sec")
# Now lets' call the xyz method
xyz()
```

Output:

```
Time taken
xyz() method takes 0.017270220561382431 sec
```

You can use cProfile on command line by running the complete program and then getting the combined time per function as output.

You can run the below script via cProfile in the command line:

```
python -m cProfile own_example.py
```

Once you run that, you will see the execution time for a list of all functions sorted by their names in ascending order. This will be pretty difficult to check where the most time has been actually spent. To overcome this, you can use sort order by using –s suffix after cProfile command.

Profiling Code

Profiling code is also related to the code's execution timing except for the fact that it determines where the time is spent. The main profiling tool used in Python is called cProfile. Please note that it is not related to IPython. cProfile helps to execute blocks of code or the complete program and keeps track of time spent on every function present in the program.

You can use cProfile on the command line by running the complete program and then getting the combined time per function as output.

You can run the below script via cProfile in the command line:

```
python -m cProfile own_example.py
```

Once you run that, you will see the execution time for a list of all functions sorted by their names in ascending order. This will be pretty difficult to check where the most time has been actually spent. To overcome this, you can use sort order by using –s suffix after cProfile command.

For example:

```
$ python -m cProfile -s cumulative own_example.py
One with the most time: 9.12572475
21376 function calls (17534 primitive calls) in 1.32 seconds
```

One thing to note here is that if a function calls another function, its timing will not stop there. It will calculate the total time required by the function until it exits from it. It will record the start time and the end time to give you the results.

cProfile not only provides the above command line function, but it can also be used to profile any code blocks without the need to start a new process. IPython provides a suitable interface with a %prun command.

```
In [ 251 ]: %prun -l 8 -s cumulative own_example()
6932 function calls in 0.738 seconds
```

The above approach by calling %run –p -s provides the same feature, but you won't have to exit the IPython interface.

Profiling a Function Line-by-Line

When %prun does not show you the entire executing time from a function, or it shows you results hard to read, like complex outputs arranged by function names, you can run a small library named line_profiler, which can be obtained from PyPI as well as package management tools.

Line_profiler has an in-built function named %lprun, which can execute the line by line profiling for the functions present in your program. To have access to this in-built function, you have to modify your IPython configuration by adding this line:

```
c.TerminalIPythonApp.extensions = ['line_profiler']
```

Although line_profiler can be used for programming, it will work in a much better and faster way when combined with IPython.

As soon as you have activated the line_profiler extension in IPython, a new command %lprun will also be available for use. The basic difference in using both of them is that you need to specify the functions to be included while using %lprun. Here is the syntax for the same:

```
%lprun -f firstFunction -f secondFunction
statement_to_profile
```

For "macro" profiling, it is advisable to run %prun (cProfile), and for "micro" profiling %lprun (line_profiling) is the best choice.

Pickles and Imports in Python

Introduction to Pickles

Pickles are one of the most useful features of Python. Pickle means to preserve or to store. In Pickle, a Python object can be represented as a string of bytes, and further, these bytes can then be saved (store) to file for later use or for transfer to another computer. Also, bytes can be transferred over a network or can be stored in a database.

To reconstitute the original Python object, these string of bytes can be unpickled. Unpickling can also be done in another instance of Python interpreter or on a different computer.

Pickle File

The most common use of pickling is to write pickle files. Pickle file contains the pickled representation of a Python Object. Pickle file contains a single object, but this single object can be a tuple or other collection of many other objects. It can be used to store temporary results for storing results as input for another Python program, writing backups, and many other purposes.

Creating a Pickle File

Below is the example for creating a pickle file from an object: in this case, a tuple containing a string, an integer, and a floating point number:

```
>>> import pickle
>>> python_object = ("hello world", 54, 23.6)
>>> pickle_file = file("test.pickle", "w")
>>> pickle.dump(python_object, pickle_file)
>>> del pickle_file
```

The dump function pickles an object to a file. In the above code, two arguments are passed in the dump function. The python_object is the object to pickle, and pickle_file is a file object to which to write the pickle.

Also, pickle_file is not written and closed until the file object is deleted.

Restoring the Pickled Data

```
>>> import pickle
>>> pickle_file = file("test.pickle")
>>> python_object = pickle.load(pickle_file)
>>> print python_object
("hello world", 54, 23.6)
```

Load function unpickles a pickle file and restores the Python object. Using the above code, pickled data can be restored. Data is loaded from the pickle file. Unpickling can be done on another computer also.

Note: The function dump returns a pickled object as a character string, and loads restores the object from a character string.

Pickling Tips

1. Basic Python data types can also be pickled: None, numbers, strings, lists, tuples, and dictionaries.

2. Since pickles can be easily ported among OS and the architectures, this enables them to pickle files easily as well as transfer them on any network of computers.

3. They are only Python Specific.

4. Pickling of compound objects can be done, including containers such as lists and tuples. Contents of container are included in the pickle.

5. If an object that has another object as an attribute is pickled, both objects are included in the pickles.

Efficient Pickling

There are two techniques for programs performing a lot of pickling and unpickling, and/or using very large pickles of large or complicated data structures.

1. The first technique uses the cPickle module for faster pickling and unpickling.

2. The second uses an alternate binary pickle protocol to write more compact pickles.

Both **pickle** and **cPickle** modules contain the same functions for pickling and unpickling, and their pickles are compatible. The difference is that pickle is itself written in Python, whereas cPickle is an extension module written in C, therefore runs much faster.

Both the modules can be used interchangeably.

For example:

```
>>> import cPickle
>>> print = cPickle.load(file("test.pickle"))
("hello world", 54, 23.6)
```

Also, both pickle and cPickle support an additional format for pickles. The default format uses ordinary text to represent objects; the alternate binary pickle protocol uses a more compact binary representation. Protocol version can be specified with an extra argument to *dump* or *dumps*.

For example:

```
>>> pickle.dump(python_object, file("test.pickle", "w"),
?)
```

Ways of Importing Modules

Python, though very clean and intuitive language, has different ways of doing things as other languages. But if you are a good python programmer, it's only one way to do a task, and that's called the "Pythonic way."

The function and variable definitions made inside the python interpreter is lost once we exit and re-enter. Hence we may want to create programs that get longer and split them into various files so that it is easy to maintain.

Python modules can be imported in two ways - *import and from-import*. Both of which are useful but cause serious confusion. Hence, a programmer should know when and how to use it and explore its subtle and important differences.

We have sorted out some of the more common issues related to *import and from-import*. Knowledge of Basic Python is required, and the reader should have used this language for some coding stuff to comprehend the differences when importing modules.

It needs Python 2.x version interpreter installed on either Windows/Unix machines.

import mod

- Imports the module *mod* into current Program memory space.

- It creates a reference to that module in the current namespace.

- No entry of the functions names defined in *mod* directly in the current symbol table. Only the module name gets stored in the symbol table as *mod.*

- <u>Permitted usage:</u> *mod.func* to refer to things defined in module *mod.*

- <u>Improper usage:</u> directly referring the function name as *func* defined in the module *mod.*

$ cat fact_mod.py

Module file fact_mod1.py computes the factorial of a given no:

def factorial(num):

```
        fact = 1
        if num == 1:
                return num
        else:
                var1 = 1
                while(var1 <= num):
                        fact = fact * var1
                        var1 = var1 + 1
                return fact
print "Successfully imported"
```

$ cat first.py

```
#!/usr/bin/python
print "hello"
import fact_mod - #Line1
factorial(4) -#Line2
```

$ python first.py

```
hello
Successfully imported
Traceback (most recent call last):
  File "first.py," line 4, in ?
    factorial(4)
NameError: name 'factorial' is not defined
```

Note that on importing the module as "import fact_mod"- *line1 *, it gives an output: <u>Successfully imported</u> meaning that the module is loaded into current namespaces, but as the function is not invoked, it doesn't execute the function definition part yet.

* Do not include the extension as .py when importing a module- it would search for a submodule py in module fact_mod.]

On execution of line2, by invoking the function present in fact_mod, it would not be recognized, as the function name is not being loaded in the symbol table. Hence, it will throw a traceback error as 'factorial' is not defined.

Correct Usage of a Function Call is in 2 Ways

```
a. # directly invoking the function with the module name
   fact_mod.factorial(5)
 120
```

```
b. # assigning a local name for the function intended to be
used quite often
fact = fact_mod.factorial
fact(5)
120
```

When importing the module itself, create an object for the module and invoke all the functions using the object name. This is similar to the above approach (b), but is not specific to a particular function of that module; it can be extended to all functions of the module. This is a better approach.

```
# fact now plays an object's role for the module/class -
fact_mod
import fact_mod as fact
fact.factorial(6)
720
```

Comparing Import Module in Python V/s other Languages

Python	import module
Perl	require module
Java	import *module*

Statements in a module will be executed only once by creating a modname.pyc file (a compiled form of Python code) irrespective of no. of times, the python module is imported. Each module has its own private symbol table, which is used as the global symbol table by all functions defined in the module. It is customary, not mandatory, to place all import statements at the beginning. Modules importing other modules are allowed in Python.

There is an alternative of the import statement which imports names from a module directly into the importing module's symbol table rather than private symbol table which is considered in next discussion now from mod import:

from mod import fns

- Imports module mod but does not introduce the mod *name* into the local symbol table.

- Creates a reference to all *public* objects defined by that module (everything except that doesn't have a name starting with "_") in the current namespace.

- Permitted usage: *func()* to refer to things defined in module *mod*.

- Improper usage: referring the function name as *mod.func* defined in the module *mod*.

```
$ from fact_mod import factorial # line1
Successfully imported

fact_mod.factorial(4)#line2
Traceback (most recent call last):
  File "<stdin>", line 1, in?
NameError: name 'fact_mod' is not defined
```

Note that on importing the module as "from fact_mod import factorial"- *line1 **, it gives an output: <u>Successfully imported</u> meaning that the module is loaded into current namespaces, but as the function is not invoked, it doesn't execute the function definition part yet.

* Do not include the extension as .py when importing a module- it would search for a submodule py in module fact_mod.]

On execution of line2, by invoking the function present in fact_mod, it would not be recognized, as the module name is not being loaded in the symbol table. Hence, it will throw a traceback error as 'fact_mod 'is not defined.

Correct usage of function call is:

```
a. # directly invoking function without module name
 >>> factorial(4)
24
```

```
b. # invoking multiple functions at a stretch
>>> from math import pow, sqrt, abs
```

Creates references in the current namespace to all the given objects a, b, c. If there are any other functions that are not imported, we will not be able to use it.

```
>>> pow (4,5)
1024.0
```

```
>>> sqrt(5)
2.2360679774997898
```

```
>>> exp(4)
Traceback (most recent call last):
  File "<stdin>", line 1, in ?
NameError: name 'exp' is not defined
# It is because exp is not imported function and not
available in the symbol table.

>>> from math import exp # import exp function now
>>> exp(5)
148.4131591025766
```

Whereas when we do "import module" irrespective whether a function is required or not, all functions loads on to your namespace.

```
c. # from module import *
```

This way of importing will load all the functions available. It may create namespace pollution. Generally, not a good idea to do until most of the functions is required.

Comparing from module import in Python V/s other languages

Python	from module import *
Perl	use module
Java	import module.*

When to use What

- Use the **import module** as a standard practice unless specified reasons as stated below.

- Accessing attributes and methods often, and don't want to type the module name multiple times, use from module import.

- Selectively import some attributes and methods, use from module import.

- Need a certain submodule from a package, convenient to write from mod.submod import fn1 instead of import mod.submod.fn1 for the same reasons that the former allows you to use just function name rather than a lengthier name as in the latter.

- The module contains attributes or functions with the same name as ones in your module; you must use import module to avoid name conflicts.

- X = __import__('X') works like import X, with the difference that you

  - pass the module name as a string

  - explicitly assign it to a variable in your current namespace

In either of the ways, each module will be imported once/interpreter session. Hence any changes done for the function/module has to undergo a restart of interpreter or reload (module).

Performance Tips

Let us see some of the performance-related tips for Python programming.

Strings

Strings in Python are immutable. It has some plus and minus.

Triple quotes ("""") are an easy way to define a string with both single and double-quotes.

```
>>> print """ABC "XYZ"etc."""
      ABC "XYZ"etc
```

String concatenation is expensive as it will create a separate object for each concatenation.

Solution:

Use percent (%) formatting

Use join() method of "str" class for concatenation

```
>>> print "XYZ" +" ABC" + ",etc"    # Don't use + operator
for concatenation
      XYZ ABC, etc
```

```
>>> print " ".join(["XYZ" ," ABC" ," ,etc"]) # Faster way of
concatenation
        XYZ ABC, etc
>>> print "%s %s %s"%("XYZ"," ABC"," ,etc")   # Another
faster way of Concatenation
        XYZ ABC, etc
```

Note: Above is applicable if your resulting string is more then 500-1000 characters long

Consider you are using OS like Windows™; there might be conflict while using the directory separators with the path string.

```
>>> import os
>>> os.path.exists('c:\\abc\\path')
```

A better way is

```
>>> import os
>>> os.path.exists(r'c:\abc\path')
```

Module Choice

cPickle is a C written module for pickle. cPickle is used to serialize python object. It is faster than pickle.

```
>>> import cPickle #, In this case, cPickle is used
everywhere is not convenience
```

If they fail to import cPickle.

```
>>> try:
        import cPickle as pickle
        except ImportError:
import pickle
```

Note: Other modules having C implementations: cStringIO for the StringIO module, and cProfile for the profile module and many more.

Importing Module

It is not necessary to import the whole module; if you require only some functions or methods, then it is better to import only the required method; otherwise, it unnecessarily loads the whole module into global-space.

```
>>> import time # it will import whole time module
>>> from time import localtime
```

We can use import statements anywhere in code. It is sometimes useful to place them inside functions to restrict their visibility. It will reduce initial startup time.

Consider the following code snippets.

```
Code Snippet1:
>>> def function1():
import string  #Import inside method
string.upper("xyz")
Code Snippet2:
>>>import string  #Import outside method
>>> def function2():
      string.upper("xyz")
```

Code Snippet2 will run much faster than Code Snippet1, even though the reference to the string module is global in Code Snippet2. Let's find out, faster method which can be easily done using timeit module:

```
>>> def function1():
        import string   #Import inside method
        string.upper("xyz")
>>> import timeit
>>> t = timeit.Timer(setup = 'from __main__ import
function1', stmt = 'function1()')
>>> t.timeit()
2.9039103556341925
>>> import string
>>> def function2():
        string.upper("xyz")
>>> t = timeit.Timer(setup = 'from __main__ import
function2', stmt = 'function2()')
>>> t.timeit()
1.3675033307938378
Code Snippet3:
>>> def function3():
        'Infy'.upper()
>>> t = timeit.Timer(setup = 'from __main__ import
function3', stmt = 'function3()')
>>> t.timeit()
0.8790898005483427
```

The above example is obviously a bit unnatural, but the general principle holds.

Note that putting an import in a function can speed up the initial loading of the module, especially if the imported module might not be required. This is generally a case of a "lazy" optimization. Lazy optimization means avoiding work, i.e. importing a module, which can be very expensive until you are sure it is required.

If the module is already loaded, then it is not loaded again.

A good way to do lazy imports is:

```
>>> string = None
>>> def function4():
        global string
        if string is None:
            import string
```

String module will only be imported once, on the first invocation of function4().

List Generators and Comprehension

List generator and comprehension expressions comes out to be pretty handy when you need to work tiny sized loops. This will make your execution much faster than for-loop.

For example:

```
>>> lstTemp = [10, 20, 30, 40, 50, 60, 70, 80, 90, 100] #
Prepare List of integers
>>> lstFinal = [x for x in lstTemp if x < 70] # Get only
items > 70
>>> lstFinal
[10, 20, 30, 40, 50, 60]
```

As shown in the above example one can use if condition to filter items.

List generator and comprehension expressions are also used when you have two or more than two lists along with zip.

```
>>> [a - b for (a, b) in zip( ( 1, 2, 3), ( 2, 3, 4 ) ) ]
[-1, -1, -1]
>>> dctTemp = { 1 : 'a', 2 : 'b', 3 : 'c'}
>>> lstTemp = [ ( x, y) for x, y in dctTemp.items()]
>>> lstTemp
[(1, 'a'), (2, 'b'), (3, 'c')]
```

Choose Data Type

It is very important to use the right data type in your Python code to create a high performance and optimized application.

Let us say that you are having two lists with you:

```
>>> lstTemp1 = [ {'a' : 1, 'b' : 2}, {'c' : 3, 'd' : 4},
{'e' : 5, 'f' : 6 }]
>>> lstTemp2 = [ {'e' : 5, 'f' : 6}, {'g' : 7, 'h' : 8},
{'i' : 9, 'j' : 10 }]
```

Now you need to find all entries which are present in both the lists. The best option to do this check is by iterating over the first list, and then checking the list item is present in the second list or not.

```
>>> common = []
>>> for entry in lstTemp1:
        if entry in lstTemp2:
                common.append(entry)
```

It will work perfectly fine for small lists where the elements are limited like 10 or 20 elements only. But this won't work for large lists having hundreds or thousands of elements in them. Therefore, in order match the common elements or items in both the lists, the below code would be fast and will give the exact result.

```
>>> setTemp1 = set([tuple(entry.items()) for entry in
lstTemp1])
>>> setTemp2 = set([tuple(entry.items()) for entry in
lstTemp2])
>>> common = setTemp1.intersection(setTemp2)
>>> common = [dict(entry) for entry in common]
```

Thus, Sets are much faster as compared to lists in these cases. You need to note than dictionaries can't come handy as members themselves because of the fact that they are mutable by nature. But that's not the case with tuples, so they can be used. Therefore, if you need to perform set operations only on dictionaries, then you first need to convert all items into tuples as well as the lists to set. Then you can perform the required operations in between and once it is done you can again convert them back. This will be much faster than replicating the set operating with the help of string functions.

Sorting

If you want to sort the lists present in the basic Python objects, it can be done in a fast manner. There is a sort() method available in Python which can take input in the form of an optional comparison function. That optional argument is then used for changing the behavior of sorting on lists. But at the same time, it might slow down the overall performance of sorts because the comparison function will be called many times. You can use the key argument to the built-in sort instead, which should be the fastest way to sort.

Let's first create an unordered list:

```
>>>   example = [5, 3, 1, 2, 4]
>>> example
[5, 3, 1, 2, 4]
```

Now performing **in-place sort** using sort() method:

```
>>> example.sort()
>>> example
[1, 2, 3, 4, 5]
```

Resetting data to its unordered state:

```
        >>> example = [5, 3, 2, 1, 4]
```

Now performing **copied sort** using sorted() method:

```
>>> exampleNew = sorted(example)
>>> example
[5, 3, 2, 1, 4]
>>> exampleNew
[1, 2, 3, 4, 5]
```

Loops

Python provides two different looping constructs. The most common loop used in Python is the for-loop. It will iterate all the items present in a sequence and then assign each item to the local loop variable. There can be a huge amount of overhead for the for-loop itself if your loop body is simple. Therefore, in such cases, the map function is pretty handy. The only thing you need to take care of in the loop body for a map is that it must be only a function call.

Let's see below example where lists of words are converted to upper case.

```
>>> newList = []
>>> for item in ["xyz","abc"]:
        newList.append(item.upper())
>>> newList
['XYZ', 'ABC']
>>> newList = map(str.upper,["xyz", "abc"])
>>> newList
['XYZ', 'ABC']
>>>
```

List comprehensions are more helpful as they are having more compact syntax and is a powerful way to write for-loop.

```
>>> newList = [s.upper() for s in ["xyz", "abc"]]
>>> newList
['XYZ', 'ABC']
```

Generator function is similar to the map or list comprehensions. The only difference is that we use it for avoiding overhead of at once generation of complete list. Its return type is an object of generator type. We can use generator object to iterate.

```
>>> newList = (s.upper() for s in ["xyz", "abc"])
>>> newList
<generator object <genexpr> at 0x0200DE90>
```

Using the most appropriate method is solely dependent on the data characteristics which you are trying to manipulate. For example, a list comprehension or a map can't be used. Then you don't have any other option but to go with the for-loop only. But the for-loop also has its limitations. Thus, you can replace the original loop with the below:

```
>>> upper = str.upper
>>> newList = []
>>> for item in ["xyz", "abc"]:
        newList.append(upper(item))
>>> newList
['XYZ', 'ABC']
```

The above technique needs to be used very carefully. If the loop becomes too large, it will be very difficult to maintain it.

Local Variables

One thing related to the for loop, if you are using a for loop, then the for-loop local variable should not be used anywhere down in the flow because it may be possible that last value can be used.

For example,

```
>>> for number in xrange(10):
        pass
>>> print number
9
```

As we can see above, the number's scope is lying outside for-loop, so if you use the same variable name, i.e. number in your later flow, then it may be possible to use wrong values for it.

The final speedup available to us for the non-map version of the for-loop, use the local variables. It is well noted fact that Python will be accessing the local variables in a much more efficient manner than the global variables.

```
>>> def toUpper():
        upper = str.upper()
        newList = []
        append = newList.append
        for item in ['XYZ', 'ABC']:
                append(upper(item))
        return newList
>>>print  toUpper()
['XYZ', 'ABC']
```

Initializing Dictionary Elements

Let us say you are going to build a dictionary having the word frequencies. First thing is to break the text into words list. Therefore, you need to execute the below code:

```
>>> dctWords = {}
```

```
>>> lstWords = ['abc', 'def', 'xyz', 'info', 'usa']
>>> for word in lstWords:
        if word not in lstWords:
            dctWords[word] = 0
        dctWords[word]+=1
```

Only apart from the first time, all other time a word will be seen when the "if" statements is false. Suppose you are counting huge amount of words, then it will be probably occurring many times. Thus, if there is a situation where value is going to be initialized only once and its augmentation will be multiple time, it is always advised to do it via a try statement only.

```
>>> dctWords = {}
>>> lstWords = ['abc', 'def', 'xyz', 'info', 'usa']
>>> for word in lstWords:
        try:
            dctWords[word]+=1
        except KeyError:
            dctWords[word] = 1
```

A very important point is to catch "KeyError" exception at an early stage and do not provide a default "except" condition to avoid recovering back from exception. It can't be handled in "try" statement.

Use xrange Instead of Range

Python has two ways to get a range of numbers: range and xrange. Most people know about range, because of its obvious

62

name. xrange, being way down near the end of the alphabet, is much less well-known.

xrange does have limitations. Specifically, it only works with integers; you cannot use longs or floats.

One thing worth noting here is that you can only have a single yielded object existing at one time. Therefore, when you are calling range, a list will be created, which will contain multiple numbers of objects like long, float, or int. All these objects will be created at a single time; thus, all exist simultaneously in the system. This is a huge drawback when you have too many numbers in your program.

But at the same time, if you will use xrange, then it will have only range objects created and not the numbers immediately. When you are pulling the generator, then only the number of objects will be created in the system.

Let us see an example:

```
>>> xrange(100000)
```

And for this reason, the code runs instantly. The functioning of both range and xrange functions is the same, but the only difference is that unlike range function xrange function does not create a list of elements directly when it is called, but only creates a range object, which can generate data when it is run in a loop.

Thus a lot of memory is saved using xrange instead of range as unnecessary no list is created.

Profiling

To make your program faster, the very first thing you need to know is where it is getting stuck for the longest amount of time. It doesn't make any sense to optimize your Python code, which is never going to be executed or is already running faster. There are two modules in Python which helps in locating the areas which are running slow and needs attention. They are profile and trace.

Using one of the profiling modules to profile executing of set of functions is a simple task. Let us say the main function which is called as main, is not taking any arguments in it. So, you want to execute the main method in the profile module. To do so, you can see the below code.

```
>>>import profile
>>> def Add():
        print 100000000 + 100000000
>>> profile.run('Add()')
200000000
        134 function calls in 0.065 seconds
```

Other

1. Decorators can be used for handling common concerns like logging, database access, pre-conditions or post-conditions, etc.

2. To stop a Python script from closing right after you launch one independently, add this code:

```
>>> print 'Press Enter to exit'
```

Press Enter to exit

```
>>> raw_input()
''
```

3. Ternary Operators:

```
[if true] if [expression] else [if false]
>>> x, y = 50, 25
>>> small = x if x < y else y
```

4. Booleans can be used as indexes:

```
>>> b = 1==1
>>> "Number is %d" % [1,2,3][b]
Number is 2
```

Gotchas in Python

Introduction

Python, though very clean and intuitive language, has gotchas as every other language. Gotcha doesn't mean a defect in language, but a situation of mismatch between the programmer's expectations of how it should work, and the way it actually works. Hence, Programmers are a Source of Gotcha(SoG) and number increases if he is from Windows/mainframe background (Cobol, Pascal, etc.) because Python is a language that evolved in a UNIX environment and incorporated a number of conventions from C family (C, C++, Java).

This chapter presents some of them:

1. Most common errors programmers do in Python

2. Proofs for - Why some things "behave so" in Python? - An answer to most of your "Why so?" questions.

3. Tips that will help you avoid being a source of gotcha! Simple and precise examples will assist the reader in understanding the concepts easily.

66

We have provided the documentation for the Python tricks and most of the gotchas, their proofs of "why they behave so" and relevant tips as and when appropriate.

Note: Some gotchas are operating system specific and to the maximum extent, have mentioned the case clearly. Users can follow it easily.

Python 2.x version interpreter installed on either Windows/Unix machines. This chapter has the Proof of concept written as 25+ Gotchas/pitfalls identified, proof explained with an example, and tips are provided.

Indentation Problem

Programmers who have been working with languages where extra whitespaces don't matter will definitely be an SoG here. Python, being an indented language, space +/- will for sure throw an **Indentation error (Windows), Syntax Error (UNIX)** with an arrow pointing to character.

Proof:

```
$ cat > poc.py
print "hello"
 print "world"
$ python poc.py
  File "poc.py", line 2
    print "world."
    ^
SyntaxError: invalid syntax
```

Tip:

Space being a character not visible on the screen, may be difficult to trace. Hence, be consistent in your indentation. Use space/ tabs consistently. Don't mix it. Any Python Editor like Eclipse can help you resolve this issue.

Missing 'print' Statement for a Variable in the File

At the interactive prompt, the habit of not providing print for expressions will be continued for a file. As a result, the output will not be as expected

Proof:

@ Interactive prompt:

```
>>> a = 10
>>> a # prints value even without having print statement
10
```

@File:

$ cat poc.py

```
print "hello"
a=10
a # just a will not work. It requires a print statement
```

$ python poc.py

```
Hello # no output for variable 'a' and surprisingly no error
also!
```

Tip: Explicit print statements are optional at interactive prompt, but **mandatory** in file.

System Commands Directly on Interactive Prompt

At the interactive prompt, habit of providing system commands directly should be avoided. Any system commands are not to be run at an interactive prompt. Python prompt will understand only Python code. Hence import the module (os, sys, etc.) and then execute commands with the help of. (Dot) operator.

Proof:

'os' is the module which helps us to execute the command as os.system(command –as a string) in a subshell. Hence use that instead of directly passing the commands from python prompt as clear, ls, etc.

```
@ Interactive prompt:
>>> print "hello"
hello
>>> clear
Traceback (most recent call last):
  File "<stdin>", line 1, in?
NameError: name 'clear' is not defined
>>> import os
>>> os.system('clear')
```

1. # clears the screen and 0 is return code if no errors were found.

On Windows: Run a Python Program by Clicking the File, and the Output Window doesn't wait for You.

Proof:

```
#!c:\python27\python.exe
print "hello"
```

Screen disappears immediately without waiting for you to see the output!

Tip:

1. Add a raw_input() at the end of the file , which shows the output and waits for you to press any key

2. If your program has any errors, to debug and fix your errors: Open the file with any interactive prompts, IDE (Eclipse, notepad, IDLE, etc.).

The Print Statement is Appending a New Line at the End

Python reference manual says by placing a comma after print, appending a newline at the end of output will be avoided.

Proof:

```
>>> for i in 'Info' : print i
...
I
n
f
o
```

```
>>> for i in 'Info' : print i, # observe the comma at the
end
...
I n f o
```

Modifing a File after Importing is Importing - not Reflecting the Changes Made

Importing at interactive prompt works **only once per session**, irrespective of the number of times you've imported! The reason is, it's referring to the module loaded earlier. To make it work for changed file: Reload the complete module

Proof:

```
$cat f1.py
      def disp(x):
              print "hello", x
      print " out of function"
$ python
>>> import f1 as F1
 out of function
>>> F1.disp(4)
hello 4
>>> import os
>>> os.system('vi f1.py')  # This will open the file in edit
mode. Make the changes and save the file.
def disp(x):
              print "hello world", x+1 # world, +1 are added
      print " out of function"
>>> os.system('cat f1.py')
def disp(x):
              print "hello world", x+1 # world, +1 are added
```

71

```
        print " out of function"
>>>F1.disp (4)
hello 4 # not reflecting changes
>>> reload(F1) # changes done will be taken care after
reloading
 out of function
<module 'f1' from 'f1.py'>
>>> F1.disp(4)
hello world  5 # changes visible
```

Module F1 will get recompiled and code is re executed, defining a new set of objects that are bound to names in the F1's dictionary.

Tip:

At the interactive prompt, if you have modified an already imported source file:

1. Reload a module – if not leaving current python interpreter session

2. Log out of prompt-> create a new session-> Import as a fresh module

Guess on Automatic Defaults for a Variable

In python, though you are given an option of using variables without its declaration (auto vivification), take a little, worthy pain of initializing a variable. To avoid guessing a variable's default value as null or 0 or empty string, etc., make your start point by initializing a variable to what you want.

Tip:

Initialize variables to 0

Lists to empty lists

Extension's During Module Import

Extensions are not required while importing a file. If extensions are provided, it will be working like you've mentioned a package name and searching for a module named after the dot(.) symbol. Though you can execute: **python /home/raj/mod.py,** whereas in import statements providing the path is not allowed like import **import /home/raj/mod.py** just because modules may have its .pyc(a compiled form of code created) and will always look into directory path from your module search path settings.

Proof:

```
>>> import fact_mod.py  #ImportError: No module named py
# will look for module named 'py' in package fact_mod
>>> import fact_mod # Valid
>>> import package.modname # valid if importing from a
package
```

Tip:

Use dot only when a file needs to be imported from within a Package.

Function Call without Parenthesis

a. Python functions should be called with parenthesis irrespective of whether they require arguments or not.

Proof a:

functionname([args]) not just functioname

Ex: f.close # succeeds with no error but will not close the file!

f.close() # closes the file

b. Functions here are simple objects. They can be assigned to any other variable also.

Proof b:

Let's assume there is a function factorial in fact_mod module.

>>> from fact_mod import factorial

>>> f=factorial # object factorial is assigned to a variable f

>>> f(3)

6

>>> factorial(5)

120

Tip:

Use object names similar to function names to avoid confusion.

Increment and Decrement Operators

There are no pre/post- increment/decrement operators in Python, unlike C/C++. Instead, you can use compound assignment operators.

Proof:

```
>>> x = 10
>>> x++ # SyntaxError: invalid syntax
>>> x+=1 # same as x = x+1
>>> x
11
```

Tip:

Be cautious about this in looping like

```
while(condition using i < 10):
        do something;    i++ # will not work
```

x+= y is not the same as x = x + y on mutable objects

x+=y is the same as changing the list in place and similar to extending a list object with the same id. Whereas x = x + y will be creating a new list and binding it to same variable x.

Proof:

```
$cat mut.py
z = [10, 20, 30]
```

```
print z, id(z)
z += [40]
print z, id(z)# same id as above
z = z + [5]
print z, id(z)
```

Output:

```
[10, 20, 30] 47370205371784
[10, 20, 30, 40] 47370205371784
[10, 20, 30, 40, 5] 47370205371856
```

Tip:

Cyclic structures are like whirlwinds and may wind your program to unexpected loops and unpredicted output. Keep track of them properly and proceed further.

Mixing Mutable and Immutable Data Structures

Mixing of immutable and mutable data structures in place is a serious pitfall in Python that is not yet fixed. Though there pops up a type error, it silently changes the mutable part of the immutable element.

Proof:

```
>>> tup1= ([1, 2, 3], 5)
>>> tup1
([1, 2, 3], 5)
>>> tup1 [0] += [6, 7] # Trying to change the list element
of a tuple
Traceback (most recent call last):
```

```
  File "<stdin>", line 1, in ?
TypeError: object does not support item assignment
>>> tup1
([1, 2, 3, 6, 7], 5)  # new elements appended to list is
successful.
```

Knowing the Range of your Sequences

Ranges operating on any sequence will be of this format

```
Datastructure[ InclusiveStart: Exclusive End:
Increment/Decremental step ]
```

Proof:

```
>>> a = "Hello World"
>>> a[:5]
'Hello'
>>> a[2:10]
'llo Worl' #From 2nd Index till 9th Index
```

Tip:

Only if the End index is less than start index, the third argument can be decremented with a negative number

Changing Immutable Elements in Place

Strings and tuples are immutable, whereas lists and dictionaries are mutable in place.

Proof:

```
>>> b = (10, 20, 30, 40) # created as a tuple
```

```
b[3]= 200 # TypeError: object does not support item
assignment
>>> b = b[:2] + (200,) # can reassign to same variable if
required
>>> b
10, 20, 200
>>> b = [10, 20, 30, 40] # created as a list
>>> b[3]= 200 # will succeed.
>>> b
[10, 20, 30, 200]
```

Tip:

Know your variable's mutable property and use the operations
accordingly.

Beware of Assign by Implicit References

Usually, when assigning a mutable element, we need to be
careful as the assignment is by reference until specified
otherwise. It is not making a copy, instead creates a reference
without informing the user.

Proof:

```
$cat list.py
x = [10, 20, 30]
y = x # y is referenced to x
z = x[:] # z is assigned with a copy of x
x.append(90)# self-referencing the same list again
print x, y, z
```

Output:

```
[10, 20, 30, 90]  [10, 20, 30, 90]  [10, 20, 30]
```

Tip:

For dictionaries dict.copy() method can be called for assigning by value.

Use of Appropriate Looping Constructs

Use of normal for loop is recommended instead of while or for with a range functions. 'for' works with implicit indexing, whereas range will create a list first and then starts the indexing with the created list. If you've to use for with a range, go for 'for' with an 'xrange' function will improve the performance during indexing.

Proof:

```
x = "Python Program"
for a in x: print a # simplest with auto indexing
# complex with unnecessary function calls
(a)   for a in range(len(x)): print x[a]
```

or

```
(b)   while a < len(x): print x[a] ; a += 1
```

Tip:

Reuse the existing simpler loops unless it is made mandate to follow logic using range.

Expecting Results from Changing Objects

Any function that changes the existing object will return none value as they modify the object and not return the modified object. Don't try to extract results out of it. Sort, reverse, insert, pop, delete, extend, etc. that work on lists and dictionary will return if assigned to a variable in place.

Proof:

```
$cat list.py
list1 = [10, 20, 30]
list1.append(90) # works fine
print list1
list1 = list1.append(40) # assigns none to original list
print list1
```

Output:

```
[10, 20, 30, 90]
None
```

Tip:

If mutable elements are modified, don't extract from in-place operations which will never return modified object but none.

Ignorant about EIBTI Rule

Python expression conversion happens on numeric data types. 10+10.4 gets added to 20.4 as the integer gets type casted implicitly to floating point and math is computed

Implicit conversion rule will not be applied on different data types like strings

Proof:

```
$cat str.py
a = '12'; b = 1
ab = a + b #TypeError: cannot concatenate 'str' and 'int'
objects
print ab
ab = a + str(b) # 121 on concatenation
#OR
Ab = int(a) + b # 13 on addition
```

Tip:

Don't forget python's EIBTI rule: Explicit Is Better than Implicit.

Default Mutable Objects behaving as Static Variables in Function Arguments

Functions defined with default argument values are evaluated and saved once when it is invoked for the first time. But, defaults retain the same object **between calls**, which may not be our requirement.

Proof:

```
$cat def_ctr.py
>>>def ctr(j = []): # creates a empty list object
... j.append(1) # add 1 every time
... print j
```

```
>>> ctr([5]) # default is hidden and uses 5 and prints [5,
1]
>>> ctr() # default is used and prints  [1]
>>> ctr() # default is used  and prints [1, 1] and keeps
growing for each call
"""To avoid behavior of static calls:
```

Assign default as none and check for any arguments passed if any during function invocation

```
"""
```

Tip:

Check if its passed else, Use classes concept to retain the state between calls.

Never use a mutable object like a list /dictionary as a default argument value. But can ignore this tip if you really know what you are doing!

Notation [...] found in your Output

If you end up referencing a collection object by itself, python will neither throw any error nor end up in infinite loop but will show a notation [...]. It has caused cyclic data structures as a loop

Proof:

```
$cat list.py
list1 = [10, 20, 30]
list1.append(90)
```

```
list1.append(list1)# self-referencing the same list again
print list1
```

Output:

```
[10, 20, 30, 90, [...]]
```

Tip:

Cyclic structures are like whirlwinds and may wind your program to unexpected loops and unpredicted output. Keep track of them properly and proceed further.

Using the Right Modes on the Right Operating Systems when Working on Files

Some operating systems treat binary and text files differently, like windows; for example, text file lines may be terminated by \r, \n, or \r\n. While reading for text files, end of the line is \n, whereas, for binary, it is \r\n. Some OS doesn't discriminate such things like, for example, on UNIX, files will be opened in binary mode. Hence python provides different explicit modes to open a file. Know it and use it.

Proof:

```
Fh1 = open(filename, "r")  # text mode
Fh2 = open(filename, "rb") # binary mode
```

Tip:

Mention the modes explicitly by following the EIBTI rule to avoid unpredicted output.

Merging many Exceptions

In case we want to write 'n' no. of exceptions in a single except block by providing a single except keyword and handling by the same block of statements, do it in a right manner. Except block accepts two arguments, first being the exception class, the second being an optional name for that class, which binds the actual exception instance that has been raised. Hence Keyerror is raised and is bound to Indexerror as a variable. Hence we don't get what we've predicted.

Proof:

```
a. >>> try:
      ...suspicious code here...
      except for Keyerror, IndexError: #expects to catch
Keyerror, IndexError- doesn't work!!
b. >>> try:
...      1/0
... except ZeroDivisionError,e:#e is the name for
zerodivisionerror
...      print e
integer division or modulo by zero
c. >>> try:
      ...suspicious code here...
      except (Keyerror, IndexError): #catches both Keyerror
,and IndexError
```

Tip:

Solution: When catching multiple exceptions in one except clause, use parentheses to create a tuple with exceptions.

UnboundLocalError:

This error occurs if a name is referring to a local variable that has not been bound.

Note: Below example of a, b, c are three independent codes

Proof:

```
a) >>> def abc():
...     a = 20 # becomes local variable
...     print a
>>> abc()
20
>>> print a # Traceback: variable not defined
b) >>> a = 20
>>> def abc():
...     print a # Variables references inside function is
global
>>> abc()
20
c) >>> def abc():
...            a = a + 20
>>> abc() # Traceback" Unboundlocalerror as variable becomes
local and is not bound
```

Tip:

Name bound in a block:: Local variable of that block

Name bound in module level:: Global Variable(Localand global)

Not defined variable in block:: Free variable

Name not found anywhere:: Raise a Nameerror exception

Name referring variable not bound:: Raise a UnboundLocalerror exception

Assigning an Expression during Condition Check

Proof:

You will not be able to write

```
while( linedata = readline(fh))
but,
while( condition):
        linedata = readline(fh) # is allowed.
```

Just to avoid the hard- to find a bug that is caused during assignment instead of comparison like in C and other scripting languages like Perl, Shell, etc.

If (a= 0) is definitely different from (a= =0). To take care of this issue and to avoid users being an SoG, python itself doesn't support assignment during condition checks.

Tip:

Go by the reference manual and don't assign while expressions during condition checks.

A few other Gotchas and Solution

1. Unnecessary semicolon at the end of the statement

   No need to place it until an executable statement is followed in the same line

2. Overlooking a colon for control structures and definition like if, while, for, def fun():

   Can fix it only by practice- No harm in accepting few initial error messages!

3. There isn't any switch case in Python as the task can be done easily with if...elif...elif...else construct only

4. For windows users: Forgetting a change to **All files** -> store with the extension **(.py)** for a code on Notepad and to avoid Automatic assignment as .txt, use user-friendly editors or remember to change it to all files and provide .py extension

5. Call to open function fh.open()on a file will look into absolute path if specified or assumes it to be relative w.r.t your directory. It will not look into Module Search Path(MSP). MSP is only referred to during module imports and not for files.

6. Floating-point no. giving high precision?

   Use str function

```
>>> f = 0.1
>>> f #0.10000000000000001
>>> str(f) # 0.1
```

Coding Standards in Python

Python is a powerful computer programming language, and it is straightforward to code in Python if you follow the coding standards specified for Python programming language. The syntax is very simple, and it allows the programmers to state their ideas in fewer lines of codes.

It is an interpreted language, and there is no compilation necessary. It is often used as a scripting language, and it is available on Windows, Mac OS, and UNIX operating systems. The variable and argument declarations are not necessary as it is determined implicitly. One major advantage of using Python is that it is platform independent and you can run it on any operating system without any issues.

Python Program

We can execute python programs in different modes of programming.

Interactive Mode Programming

```
$ python
```

```
Python 2.4.3 (#1, Nov 11 2019, 13:34:43)
[GCC 4.1.2 20080704 (Red Hat 4.1.2-48)] on linux2
Type "help", "copyright", "credits" or "license" for more
information.
>>>
```

Type the following text at the prompt and then use the enter key
–

```
>>> print "Hello, World!"
```

If you are running a new version of Python, then you would need
to use print statement with parenthesis as in print ("Hello,
Python!");

However, in Python version 2.4.3, this produces the following
result –

```
Hello, Python!
```

Script Mode Programming

Calling program by using python <file name>

In script mode .py files are   run in the Python interpreter.

Instead of using to run one/multiple line or block of code at a
time, we can type up all your code in one text file, or script, then
execute all the code at once.

Steps:

- Open the Python shell prompt

- Next "File -> New File" [OR] hit Ctrl + N)

- Paste your code into a new window

- save the script with a **".py"** extension

- Next, go to "Run" -> "Run Module" [OR] press F5

For example:

```
def sample_script ():
a = 3
b = 4
c = a + b
print (c)
```

Save above code with **sample_script.py** and follow the above steps.

Python File Extensions

py -The normal extension for a Python source file

pyc- The compiled bytecode

pyd- A Windows DLL file

pyo- A file created with optimizations

pyw- Python script for Windows

pyz- Python script archive

Statements in Python

Every statement is isolated with End of Line (Press Enter in the script). Statement can be anything from assigning a value to reading the input or writing the output on the screen.

Python is a case sensitive language. (E.g. ABC is not similar to abc). Therefore, if we declare a variable with capital letters, then it will not identify it a later stage in the code with small case letters.

For example:

```
x = 1
y = 2
z = 3
```

Identifiers

Identifier is a name that we use for identifying the different variables, classes, methods, objects, etc. in a program. Each identifier name has to be unique and can't be used twice in the program for declaration of variables, classes, or methods.

The basic rules to create an identifier are:

1. It should start with small case a to z or capital case A to Z, or with underscore sign (_). After assigning the first letter, you can use digits as well from 0 to 9.

2. Special characters like \$, @, % are not allowed to be used in the identifiers.

3. An identifier is case sensitive. Therefore, identifier name **Salary** and **salary** are considered as two different ones in the Python programming language.

4. You can't use a reserved word as an identifier in Python, such as break, class, while lambda, for, from, print, raise, etc.

Now let us see some naming conventions while creating identifiers in Python.

1. All Class names will start with A-Z. Remaining identifiers can be written as a-z. For example, Employees, Students, and Country.

2. If the identifier starts with a single underscore, it means that it is a private identifier.

3. If the identifier starts with a double underscore, it means that it is a strong private identifier.

4. If the identifier ends with a double underscore, it means that it is a language-specific identifier name.

Indentation

It defines the code line alignments, tabs, spaces, etc....

As we know that curly braces are not used in Python for delimiting the code, therefore using correct syntax in Python is very important. You need to properly indent your Python code under loop, class, or function.

Indentation is possible by using spaces or tabs, or both. One thing worth noting here is that indent statements present inside a code block must have the same number of spaces and tabs in it.

Line Structure

When we use a newline token, it will follow each logical line written in thePythonprogram. Python's inbuilt interpreter is pretty smart, and it will automatically ignore the blank lines on its own.

```
# Python syntax
print (" Hi, how are you guys")
```

Below lines will cause the error in the program.

```
# Python syntax
print (" Hi,
how are you guys")
```

Multiline Statements

Python has no support for semicolons, and thus every new line will be treated as a new statement in Python. Suppose there is a requirement to split the statements into more than two lines, then it can be done using the below methods.

By using Backward Slash

```
print ("Hello\
how are you?")
More examples:
z\
=\
99
print(z)
```

Using Triple Quotes in a String

```
print (""" Hello guys how are you?""")
More examples:
 """z\
=\
10"""
print(z)

# it will cause an error
```

Comments

Comments are used to write the meaning or purpose of the statement. The python interpreter can ignore comments during the runtime. They are very handy to give details about the logic performed in your code for other readers. It ensures that other programmers who are reading your code will understand it easily.

\#   is used to comment a single statement

""" """ is used to comment multiple statements

Examples:

```
# Python syntax
## print (" Hi, how are you guys")
### print (" Hi, how are you guys")
# print (" Hi, how are you guys") #
count = 0   # initializing count with zero


"""
i = 1
j = 2
k = 3
"""
```

Using Blank Lines

If we leave a line with just whitespace known as blank line and the interpreter will ignore it.

Multiple Statements

Set multiple statements in python on **one line** by using a semicolon (;)

For example:

```
>>> s = 33; print(s)
>>> if 9 > 3: print ("9")
```

Multiple Statement Groups as Suites

A bunch of statements, which form a single code block are called suites.

Here is an example:

```
if expression1:
    suite1
elif expression2:
    suite 2
else:
    suite3
```

Variables

The variables are used to store data in a programming language. We can directly define any variable in python, and there is no declaration required for variables. In other words, python does not allow declaring variables with data types. There are many types of variables like Boolean, Character, Integer, Float, String, etc.

```
x = 10
print(x)
x = 'Hello'
print(x)
```

The = operator is used for assignment of the right value to the variable on the left. Python includes the following basic variable types:

- Numbers

- String

- List

- Tuple

- Dictionary

Numbers

Storing a value in a variable is not enough. It is necessary to process the value of having a useful program. The functions or operators in Python are used for this purpose. Basic operators in Python are:

- sum

- difference

- product

- division

It is possible to apply these operators to variables or the numbers directly. The following example shows how to apply the math operations on the numbers directly.

For example:

```
>>> 2.5 + 3
5.5
>>> 2.5 - 3
-0.5
>>> 2.5 * 3
7.5
>>> 2.5 / 3
0.83
```

It is also possible to mix a variable and a number:

For example:

```
>>> x = 2.5
>>> x + 3
5.5
>>> x - 3
-0.5
>>> x * 3
7.5
>>> x / 3
0.83
```

String

String types are used to store series of characters as shown in Example below. Note the quotation marks around the characters, which is used to indicate the compiler to interpret this character set as a string. There are operators that works strings. It is possible to use basic math operators on strings as well.

In Python, string is identified by the characters in quotes such as single ('') and double (""). They can only store character values and is a primitive datatype. Please note that strings are altogether different from integers or numbers. Therefore, if you declare a string "111", then it has no relation with the number 111.

For example:

```
>>> x = "abc"
>>> x + "d" abcd
>>> x * 3
abcabcabc
```

The + operator is used for concatenation of two strings and the * operator is used for repetition. It is possible to slice the strings:

For example:

```
>>> name = "John Brown"
>>> name[0]
"John"
>>> name[ 0 : 4 ]
"John"
>>> name[ 5 : 10 ]
"Brown"
>>> name[5:]
"Brown"
```

Note that the indexing starts from 0, i.e. the first letter is accessed by x[0].

The string index starts from 0 in Python.

```
>>> word = 'hello'
>>> word[0]
'h'
>>> word[2]
'l'
```

Indices may also be negative numbers, to start counting from the right. Please note that **negative indices** start from -1 while **positive indices** start from 0 (since -0 is the same as 0).

```
>>> word = 'good'
>>> word[-1]
'd'
>>> word[-2]
'o'
```

The slicing in Python is used to obtain substring, while index allows us to obtain a single character.

```
>>> word = 'develop'
>>> word[ 0:2 ]
'de'
>>> word[ 2:4 ]
've'
```

Please note that the **starting** position is always included, and the **ending** position is always excluded.

```
D  e  v  e  l  o  p
0  1  2  3  4  5  6 ---- Index value
```

In the above example, the word is assigned a value develop. Considering the first statement word [0:2], the output is 'de.'

Here the starting position 'd'(0th index) is included, and the ending position 'v' (2nd index) is excluded. Similarly, in the second statement word [2:4], the starting position 'v' (2nd index) is included, and the ending position 'l' (4th index) is excluded.

The important point to be noted in strings that Python **strings are immutable** (i.e., Strings cannot be changed).

There are many in-built functions available with String. They are used for various purposes. Let's see some of the basic ones which are used mostly.

- Len: It is the length function that is used to calculate the number of characters present in the string.

- Lower: It will convert all the uppercase characters present in the string to lowercase letters. Therefore, after using this function, all characters in the string will be in lowercase only.

- Upper: It will convert all the lowercase characters present in the string to uppercase letters. Therefore, after using this function, all characters in the string will be upper case only.

- Split: It helps to split the string into parts by using a delimiter. It can be separated using spaces, new lines, commas, or tabs.

Reading Input and Printing

Python has two important functions for printing the variables and reading them from keyboard, namely: print(), input(). An example that reads the user's name and prints given below:

For example:

```
name = input("What is your name?")
surname = input("What is your surname?")
print("Your name is: " + name + surname)
```

The program asks the user for his/her name and surname, then prints the combined name immediately.

The following program is a metric converter from centimeters to inches

For example:

```
cm_inch = 0.3937
cm = input("Enter a value in cm.: ")
cm = double(cm)
inch = cm * cm_inch
print(f"{cm} centimeters is {inch} inches")
```

String Manipulation

We can use built-in functions to manipulate strings in python. The package "string" provides more functions on strings.

For example:

```
print name = "ABCD XYZ xyz"
```

print len(name)	# It will return the length of the string name
print list(name)	# It will return the list of characters in name print
name.startswith('A')	# It will return True if name starts with A else returns False
print name.endswith('Z')	# It will return True if name ends with Z else returns False
print name.index('CD')	# It will return the index of CD in name
print 'C'.isalpha( )	# It will return True if C is alpha or returns False
print '1'.isdigit( )	# It will return True if 1 is digit or returns False
print name.lower( )	# It will return a string with lowercase characters in name
print name.upper( )	# It will return a string with uppercase characters in name

The Range Function

Python has a built-in function called *range()*. It is very commonly used with *for*-loops. It tells Python to traverse through the specified range in the list. The *range()* function generates a list of integers with the specified range. An important thing to remember is the *range()* function in Python is zero-based like the index, which means that it starts to count from 0.

Python's Range Parameters

Python's *range( )* function can take up to three parameters. Each parameter it takes serves a different purpose. They are generally defined as *stop, start,* or *step.*

Single Parameter

When the function is holding a single parameter, it is holding the *stop* parameter. So with range (stop), stop would be stopping number. Recall that the range function starts from 0, which means it would create an array of whole numbers that start from 0 up to the stopping number but not including the stopping number. So *range(n)* would generate a list of integers from *0* to *n-1*.

Syntax

```
range(stop)
```

Here is an example to help you understand the concept better.

TASK: Print numbers from 0 through 10.

There are multiple ways to obtain the desired result. Let's go over the possible solutions for the above problem from what we have learned so far.

One of the ways to do would be to write out 11 separate print statements. Another way to do so would be to use a counter with a while loop. We could also just use the for loop to print the numbers out, or we could use the range( ) function with the for-loop.

Let's first try and write the code using just the for loop without the range( ) function. We would first need to declare a list with all the numbers and then traverse through the list using the loop.

```
# declaring the list.
x = [ 0, 1, 2, 3, 4, 5, 6, 7, 8, 9, 10]
for each in x:
        print(each)
```

This would then produce the following result.

```
0
1
2
3
4
5
6
7
8
9
10
```

Now let us try to achieve the same result using the range( ) function. This time we do not need to write the entire list of numbers. We could simply declare a variable for the range function.

```
i = range(11) # This creates a list 'l' that holds numbers 0
through 10.
```

```
for each in i: # We now use the for loop to print each
number in the list.
      print(each)
```

Now try running the above code. It executes the same result as it did before. The range( ) function simplifies a programmer's job.

Note that we use range(11) to print numbers 0 through 10. Remember that range( ) function is zero-based. So range(11) would print numbers up to 11 but **not** 11.

Double Parameters

So what do we do if we wanted to start at one instead of 0?

Another method to use the *range( )* function is by passing two parameters to the function. When the function reads only two parameters, it reads them as the *start* and *stop* parameters. The *start* parameter tells the computer where the sequence would **start** and *stop* tells it where to **end.** Remember, it only goes up to the *stop* parameter, but does **not** include the same.

Syntax

```
range(start, stop)
```

TASK: Print numbers from 1 through 10 using the *range( )* function.

Our approach would be very similar to the previous one. Only this time, we add a *start* parameter. Let us write the code using this, and see what results we obtain.

```
# Declaring a variable that will hold the list with the
specified range.
x = range (1, 11) # 1 is the starting integer, and 11 would
define the stopping point.
# The list will not include 11.
        for each in x:
        print (each)
```

When you run the above code, it produces the following result.

```
1
2
3
4
5
6
7
8
9
10
```

Notice that it starts to print from 1 up to 10, but does **not** include 11.

Triple Parameters

What if I wanted to print all even numbers between 1 and 10?

Python's *range( )* function can take up to three parameters. So when the function is passed three parameters, it reads them as *start, stop*, and *step* in that order. We already learned what the *start* and *stop* parameters do. The *step* parameter is the difference between each number in the sequence.

Syntax

```
range(start, stop, step)
```

TASK: Print all even numbers between 1 and 10 using the *range( )* function.

Now, think about the solution for a minute. We need to print only the even numbers. We know that the first even number is 2, and we also know that the difference between two consecutive even numbers is 2.

```
# Our list would start at 2, and the stopping parameter
would be 11.
# The step parameter would be 2.
x = range(2, 11, 2)
#Now writing our for-loop.
for each in x:
      print(each)
```

Now execute the above code. The result displayed should be as follows.

```
2
4
6
8
10
```

Iterating by Sequence Index

Python allows us to use the index of elements to iterate a given sequence. The element's index is used as a counter in loops. Let's take a look at an example.

TASK: In the list provided, print the first five numbers in the given list. Be sure to use a loop and the sequence index to obtain your result. a = [21, 22, 24, 25, 27, 23, 25, 27, 14].

```
a [21, 22, 24, 25, 27, 23, 25, 27, 14]
for an index in range (5): #, we pass 5 as the parameter
because we only need the first five.
        print(a[index])
```

This should produce the following result.

```
21
22
24
25
27
```

If –Else Statement

The if-else statement is used to make the choices from 2 or more statements. It comes helpful when you want to execute a particular statement based on a True or False condition.

The syntax of if statement is:

If condition:

```
    action-1        # Indentation
```

```
Else:
    action-2          # Indentation
```

Here the **indentation** is required. The actions action-1 and action-2 may consist of many statements but they must be all indented.

```
if <expression> :
        <statements>
else :
        <statements>
```

The example is shown below.

```
>>> e = 6
>>> f = 7
>>> if(e < f):
...     print( 'f is greater than e' )
... else:
...     print(' e is greater than f')
...
Output: f is greater than e
def  numberProperty1 ( input ) :
        if input % 2 ==  0 :
print input , ' is an Even number '
        else :
print input,' is an Odd number '
numberProperty1( 10 )    # result is 10 is an Even number
numberProperty1( 11 )    # result is 11 is an Odd number
```

Nested If

It consists of more than 2 statements to choose from.

```
def numberProperty2 ( input ) :
      if input < 0:
            print input , ' is a Negative number '
      elif input == 0:
            print input , ' is Zero '
      else:
            print input , ' is a Positive number '


numberProperty2 ( -100 )   # -100  is a Negative number
numberProperty2 ( 0 )                # 0  is Zero
numberProperty2 ( 100 )    # 100  is a Positive number
```

Functions

A function is a block of organized and reusable code that is used to perform related activities. We can break our huge lines of programming code into smaller modules with the help of functions. It also helps in avoiding the repetition of code as we don't need to write the same lines of code again and again. Instead, we can write it once inside a function and then use the function anywhere in the program.

You need to make sure that the function name is unique.

Rules to define a function in Python:

1. In Python, function is defined using the keyword def.

2. The arguments will be placed within the parenthesis ().

Now let us see an example for the same:

```
>>> def printdetails(name, age):
...       print "Name:", name;
...       print "Age:", age;
...       return;
...
>>> printdetails(name = "Mary", age = 30);
Name: xxx
Age: 30
```

In the above example 'printdetails 'is the function name and name and age are the parameters.

Syntax of User Defined Method

```
def    < function name> :
       [ < declaration of local variables > ]
       [ < statements > ]
```

Now let us see an example for the same:

```
Language = "Python"
def printString( input ) :
      print input
def multiply ( x, y ) :
      return x * y
def power( x, y):
      return x ** y
printString( Language )        # returns Python
z = multiply( 10, 20 )
print z                # returns 200 which is equal to 10 * 20
print power( 10, 2 )   # returns 100 which is equal to 10 **
2
```

Accepting Inputs during the Runtime

raw_input() is a built-in python function provides the facility to accept input during the execution of the script

Now let us see an example for the same:

```
name = raw_input( "\n Please enter your name : " )
```

This statement provides a message to the user to provide input for name.

Docstrings

It is the documentation string, and it is used for explaining the code. It is similar to the comments, but they are a bit different when it comes to being more specific in nature. Moreover, they will be getting retained even at the runtime of your Python code. This will help the developer to inspect the docstrings when code is running. You can easily delimit the docstring with the help of 3 double-quotes. It can be put in the first line of a function to describe the working.

Triple Quotes

```
def func ():
"""This function prints out a greeting"""
print ("Welcome to my team!!")
func ()
```

Single Quotes

```
def func ():
'''This function prints out a greeting'''
print ("Welcome to my team!!")
func ()
```

Access Docstring at Runtime

By using the __doc__ built-in attribute, we can display the docstring at runtime.

```
def func ():
    """This function prints out a greeting"""
    print ("Welcome to my team!!")
print (func. __doc__)
```

Waiting for the User

The below code of the program is useful for making a program to wait for user input.

```
Numb1 = int (input ("Enter value for number1: ="))
Numb2 = float (input ("Enter value for number2: ="))
```

Command Line Arguments

These are instructions given to a program/script at runtime, by using this arguments programmers can run the programs.

The script name and additional arguments are passed to the script in the variable "sys.argv" (sys is a module and argv is a list in python). They are very important to perform the system configuration tasks.

Single space ( ) isolates the arguments in the command line.

"print" is used to print statements in the console.

python -h

```
usage: python [option] ... [-c cmd | -m mod | file | -]
[arg] ...
```

For example:

```
import sys
print "Argument number zero: ", sys.argv[ 0 ]
print "Argument number One: ", sys.argv[ 1 ]
print "Argument number Two: ", sys.argv[ 2 ]
print "Argument number Three: ", sys.argv[ 3 ]
```

Execute the script in the below-mentioned syntax.

```
python commandline.py Zero One Two Three
```

Creating your First Program in Program

Introduction

Pycharm: we need first to install pycharm in our system to create any program or code in Python. This is a platform editor and was developed by Jet Brains. It provides many useful tools that will be needed for Python code development.

Steps for Writing a Python Program

1. Pycharm editor needs to be open first. Now we will see the introductory screen.

2. For the creation of a new project, we will click on 'Create New Project.'

3. We need to select a location where we want to create the project. Later if we need to change the name from "untitled" to some other like "MyFirstProject."

4. Click on the 'Create' button.

5. Select the 'File' menu then New. Then we will select 'python file.'

6. When we select the file, then a pop up will appear. We need to write or type the name of the file which we want like "Hello World" and then click on 'OK.'

7. Now we will write a program to print ('Hello World').

Code:

```
print ('Hello World').
```

8. Now navigate to the "Run" menu, and we will select "Run" to run our program in the editor.

9. We will check the output of our program at the editor's screen.

10. Note: If we haven't installed Pycharm Editor in our system then, we will use the command prompt to run the program. We need to enter the correct path of a file (.py) in command prompt, which will run the code program.

11. Write the below in command prompt

```
C:\>cd PycharmProject>HelloWorld.py (running python
code from the command prompt)
```

Output:

```
Hello World
```

Below is the explanation of the Main function in Python.

```
[def main ():]
Taking an example:
```

```
def main():
    print "Hello World"
print "Hello"
```

There are two statements for printing the lines in the above code.

First print statement is defined inside the main function, which is "Hello World." The second print statement, "Hello" is not inside the main function and thus is an independent line.

Now we will run the def main () method and see what does it print.

Output would be:

"Hello" gets print out but not "Hello World"

This has happened because we have not provided the declaration for the call function. It should be:

"if __name__ == "__main__"

Here python interpreter is reading the source file and will be executing every line of code which is present there.

Now when it runs that source file to be a program, it will first set the special variable called __name__, and that will be having a value "__main__."

Here we are executing the main function, so now it reads the "if" statement. It will be checking whether _name_ is equal to _main_.

Python "if__name__== "__main__" allow us to run files as standalone programs.

Once we have defined the main function, we will be calling the code by if__name__== "__main__". Once it is done, then code will be run, then only we will be getting output "Hello World" in the console:

```
def main():
  print("Hello World")
if __name__ == "__main__" :
  main()
print("Hello")
```

Output would be:

```
"Hello World" gets print out but not "Hello"
```

Installing Python with Django and Selenium in Eclipse

Python Setup on Windows

- Visit the official python website

- Navigate via the downloads tab to the downloads for windows

- Click the button to begin downloading the latest python 3 version

- Click on the downloaded file and select "Run the installer."

- After the installer starts, ensure that the "Add python to PATH" option is selected.

- Click on "Install Now"

- You may be warned to allow the python installer to make changes to your computer, which you should accept.

- After a few minutes, the installer will complete, after which you should close the installer.

Verifying your Python Installation

- Start the Windows PowerShell

- Type python at the prompt

- You will be taken to the "Triple arrow point," which indicates that python is waiting for your input.

- Welcome to Python!!

What is Django?

Django is a web framework for Python. Although there are almost twenty python frameworks for making web applications or websites, these may be categorized into a low level or the high level. Among all, Django is the highest level of all. It is built on top of Python to make websites. This framework is still under active development. Every website in Django is a combination of certain applications. The features and characteristics of Django are discussed below.

In this document, backend development in Python or working with databases is explained, not working with JavaScript or any kind of front end technology.

Features of Django

- **High-Level Python Web framework**: Django can be compared to another framework available in python, like flask. Flask is low level. This means you can customize the folder structure in your own way. Various flask apps may look different from each other. You can design your app in a way you like, but it may or may not be the best way.

  On the flip side, Django provides you almost certainly the best way to design the app. But one has to follow the Django way to implement the project. There is comparatively less freedom as compared to low-level frameworks, but the project will certainly be less messed up. You will not end up making anything onerous. That's called a high-level framework. There are various frameworks in Python; Django is probably the highest one in terms of levels. It's a good start for beginners.

- **Free and Open Source**: It's a free and open-source available for various OS.

- **Encourages rapid development**: It is suitable for getting things up and running quickly. It is designed for developing apps in a burgeoning manner.

- **Follows MTV (Model Template View) Design pattern**: Django is not completely an MVC framework. However, it is sometimes referred to as an MVC design. Rather it's an MTV framework. The 'C' (Controller) is its inbuilt functionality. Django is heavily influenced by MVC though.

In MVC, the controller handles the requests and routes it to the business code at the backend, and it is also responsible for showing the correct view sent from the backend to the front end users. The Views are what shown to the users, and the model is in the data access layer. Just like MVC, MTV has the data access layer in the Model. Anything to do with interacting, relating the data or validating the data, that's all going to go into the model. The Template is the presentation layer. So our presentation-related decisions go here, like how things should be displayed on the web page, or whatever type of document should be shown.

And at last, the business logic layer is the V layer, it accesses the models directly and displays the appropriate template. So the View works kind of like a View Controller, and that's a bridge between the models and the templates. A lot of which the controller handles in the MVC is actually handled here by the View. So that is the biggest difference between how

Django works and how traditional MVC frameworks are like, e.g. Ruby on Rails.

- **The concept of Apps**: Another unique thing about Django is that it uses the concept of apps. You can imagine a single project as an app, but in Django, every project or website can have multiple apps inside it. It may also have a single app. For example, you can have a blog app, client app to handle your client functions or the store app, and so on.

  You can also move apps from one project to another pretty easily, and you can use other people's apps. So this whole setup is very flexible and scalable and reusable.

Why Django?

- **Rapid Development**: It was designed for rapid development. You can get the entire backend administration system for your models in minutes, and every model you create is very simple to add to that backend.

- **Full-featured**: Django is full-featured and fully loaded. It has a ton of functionalities in its core, like user authentication, administration, etc.

- **High Performance**: In terms of its size and performance, it is a very efficient framework. It performs pretty well as compared to other frameworks.

- **Highly Secure**: It protects you from things like SQL injection, cross-site scripting attacks, and cross side forgery. Many different websites use this framework like Instagram, Pinterest, Disqus, Nasa, Firefox Help Site, etc. It is highly secure and provides user authentication as an inbuilt feature.

- **Scalability:** Can handle a large number of users, and also, the Django project is itself scaled, i.e., it can have various different applications in a single project. It can hold a lot of traffic.

- **Versatile:** It's a versatile language used to build many different kinds of websites, from social networking websites and content management systems to things like scientific computing platforms. And as it runs on Python, which is itself very powerful and versatile language in itself.

Python Virtual Environment

The last thing which can be discussed about Django before going to work on it is that Python has a virtual environment, which gives you a virtual environment for all its python instances. That's a recommended way to use Django. It's not necessary, but a good way to work on Django. It can create isolated environments with their own directories.

This used to be very difficult to use on Windows, but it's much simpler now.

Installing Django

1. **Installing Python:** Django runs on Python. So before installing Django you would require Python in your system. You can get the latest version from https://www.python.org/downloads/.

Make sure that the Django version you want to use should be appropriate for the python version on your system.

With the latest Django version, it is recommended to use Python 3. For applications based on Python 2.7, Django 1.11 is required. But the support for this version of Django for Python 2.7 is going to end in 2020.

2. **Installing pip:** While installing python, make sure that you are installing pip, which is a python package manager.

You will need it to install Django later. Your folder structure should look like below.

And pip should reside in the Scripts folder.

3. **Verify Python Installation**: Once you install python in your system, you can verify it by checking its version from the command line. Firstly, you need to add to the Path in the environment variables to access it anywhere in your system.

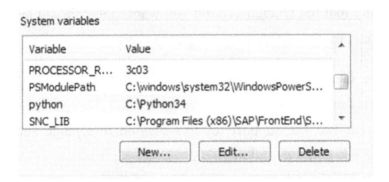

Now type python in the command line, and it checks if it installed or not.

4. **Installing Django:** Type below command in the directory of Scripts folder where pip is downloaded.

```
pip install django
```

It will install the latest Django framework for you. But if you want to install a particular version, for instance, if you want to have 1.9 Django on your system, then mention the Django version in the command itself.

```
pip install Django = 1.9
```

5. **Verify Django:** By typing python command in cmd, and then importing python and checking the version by using below commands:

```
-import django
-print(django.get_version())
```

Note: You may need to uninstall the older version of Django first, if any, to install a newer version. Also, if pip is outdated, then firstly upgrade it; otherwise, it is not going to work while installing Django.

Now you are ready to make a basic Django application.

Working on Django

1. **Adding django-admin to environment variables:** The Python folder has the script folder inside it, as shown above, in which there is an executable file by the name of django-admin.

You first need to add it to the Path in environment variables to use it anywhere in your system.

2. **Creating a Django project:**

Open the cmd in the directory you want to create the project.

Type command – "django-admin startproject project_name"

You will see that a project has been created in that directory.

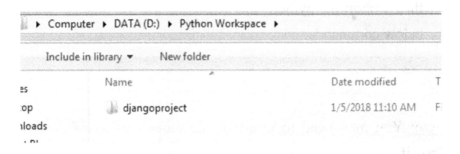

3. **Project Structure:** Project folder initially contains a manage.py file and another folder with the same name, which further contains four different python files.

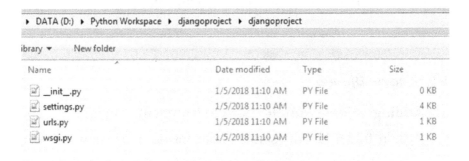

4. **Significance of the above files:** Django has its own project structure, unlike flask, where you can customize things. The outer project name, i.e., djangoproject in our case, can be renamed to any other name. It acts as a container for the whole inner project. Below is the significance of these files in a Django project:

   i. **manage.py:** To interact with your Django project, this manage.py file acts as a command-line utility. It has various commands like runserver, createsuperuser, makemigrations, testserver, check, etc.

ii. **__init__.py:** It is just an empty file to tell Python that this folder/directory is to be taken as a Python package.

iii. **settings.py:** It has all the settings/configurations required for the application, like middleware settings, database settings, or the apps inside the project.

iv. **urls.py:** This file contains the URLs and the declarations. Each URL will be pointing to some methods inside the project.

v. **wsgi.py**: This python file serves as the entry point for web servers compatible with WSGI.

5. **Verifying Django Project:** Let us now verify that the project structure created above works fine or not. Go to the project, in the outer "djangoproject" directory and open the command line and type below command:

```
python manage.py runserver
```

It will start the server at default path http://127.0.0.1:8000/, which is your localhost at port number 8000.

This is a light-weighted web server. It's written in pure Python. However, it is only suitable for development purposes, not for production usage like apache tomcat or any other server.

Browse to the above path, and you will see a webpage just like below:

You can also provide an IP and a port in the command itself to start the server at the desired address and port.

    i.   **Changing port only** : type command - **python manage.py runserver [port number]**

    ii.   **Changing ip/port:** type command - **python manage.py runserver [ip:port]**

For instance, **python manage.py runserver 0:8080.**

Here, 0 is an abbreviation for 0.0.0.0

If you need to make certain code changes, then it will not require a server restart. This dev server automatically reloads the whole code as needed, whenever a request is made. However, if you are adding files to your project, then it may certainly require a restart.

Also, you will notice that the directory of manage.py will now have another file "db.sqlite3", which is created after running the server. This is an internal database used by Django. Let's not think about the database for now and ignore the "unapplied migrations" warning in the command line.

Creating a Django app

After following the above basic steps to create a python project structure and learning about the directories and the development server, let us now create an application inside this project.

Use manage.py to start an app inside your project as in the example below:

```
python manage.py startapp [app_name]
```

```
D:\Python Workspace\djangoproject>python manage.py startapp djangoapp
D:\Python Workspace\djangoproject>
```

Notice the djangoapp is created in the same directory where manage.py resides.

So this is how Django works.

Installing Python Selenium in Eclipse

Introduction

Python is a powerful language for scripting and application development. It is mainly suitable for developing full-fledged applications. But Python can also be used to automate your normal window web-browser for testing purposes. This explains how to install and configure Python Selenium in Eclipse.

Prerequisites

- Make sure you have installed **Eclipse** on the machine.

- Make sure you have installed **Python** on the system.

- Make sure you have **chromedriver.exe** in your system(The latest **chrome driver** can be downloaded from "**https://chromedriver.storage.googleapis.com/index.ht ml**")

Installing Selenium in Python:

Step1: Installing Pip in Python

Copy all the contents from "https://bootstrap.pypa.io/get-pip.py" to notepad and save it as **get-pip.py** in python installed folder (where python.exe is present, in my case I have kept it in "**C:\Python27**" path)

Run command in Command Prompt from python folder.

python get-pip.py

This command will use **get-pip.py** file and install pip in existing python

Step2: Installing selenium in Python
Once pip is installed Script folder will be created in the Python folder, and you can locate pip.exe in the Script folder.

Open Command Prompt from this location and run command
pip   install   –U   selenium
This Command will install Selenium Python in your python. To make sure it's installed, you can find selenium folder in "**Python27\Lib\site-packages**" this path.

Installing Python Selenium in Eclipse:
Step1: Install PyDev package in Eclipse
Download and install package from the Eclipse
Help > Eclipse_Marketplace > Search:PYDEV > Install PyDev

You can also download packages manually and install them from "https://sourceforge.net/projects/pydev/files/pydev/."

Step2: Restart Eclipse If it was running.

Step3:   Select   Python   Interpreter   in   Eclipse
Go   to   Window>Preferences   >   PyDev   >   Interpreters   >
PythonInterpreter>New
Add the path of python.exe from your machine.

Step4: Create a Python Project and Python Module you should be now able to create a Python project, create a new module, and start scripting.

Sample Scripts:

```
from selenium import webdriver
driver = webdriver.Chrome("path of chrome driver")
driver.get("http://www.google.com")
assert "google" in driver.title
driver.close()
```

Different Versions of Learning Python

Here we can get an overview of Python programming and its latest version Python 3.0 and the comparison of python 3 with its previous versions and the brief description of the various operating systems where python can be used.

The following is the C style code:

```
if (a = 1)
{
        if (b! = 1)
{
  fun1()
        {
                fun2()
        }
```

The python style code is as below:

```
if a = 1:
```

```
if b! = 1:
fun1()
fun2()
```

Varieties of Python Implementation

There are few other python implementations like:

1. CPython and Jython are Python for the Java environment

2. Python with a JIT compiler

3. Python for .NET and the CLR

4. Python 3 is a new version of Python. It will be replacing the Python 2.x

Differences between Python 3.x and Python 2.x:

1. The print statement is now known as a print function.

2. By default, Strings are made Unicode.

3. All the classed are now following the new style.

4. To catch the expressions, the syntax has been changed.

5. Division of integers is now converted to result in a float value only. Earlier it was resulting in an integer value.

6. Long integer has been made obsolete, and I longer available.

Interactive Python

Giving an interactive prompt is a special feature in python when executed without arguments in the command line. Coding in python can be started by just typing python in the command prompt, as shown below:

```
$ python
Python 2.6.1 (r261:67515, Jun 07, 2018, 15:19:23)
[GCC 4.3.2] on linux2
 Type "help", "copyright", "credits" or "license" for more
information.
>>> print 'Hai'
 >>> Hai
```

Python prompts with the symbol '>>>'

Evaluation of inputs in python

```
>>>3*(2 + 3)
15
```

Command used to exit from prompt

CTRL+D

Naming conventions in python:

- Names in python are case sensitive

- Identifiers cannot start with a number

- Numbers, underscores, and letters can be used in python

```
Ex: mob, _mob, mob_2 etc.
```

Python on Different Operating Systems

Linux Ubuntu:

The command-line version is pre-installed so that it makes it easy for installation. We can also implement python using a graphical interactive development environment (IDLE) or command-line version.

Program using the command line:

To run a program in command line –

```
>>> python my_sample.py
```

To exit from the command line type CTRL + D

Sample code using Python Linux:

To start with a python code in IDLE go to File -> New window, which opens a note pad or text editor.

Code:

```
#linuxversion.py
#User input version and print response
name = raw_input ("Enter the Linux version you use?")
print "I use," name, " - Linux!"
```

Output:

```
Enter the Linux version you use?
Ubuntu
I use Ubuntu - Linux!
```

The user input can be taken by using a keyword called *"raw_input."*

Save the source code file with .py extension and execute the program using Run ->Run module from the menu.

Python on Android

Since python is a platform-independent language, it can be used with different operating systems and Android is one of the operating systems

Before starting, pre-requisite is to have an **Android SDK** and **Java SDK**

Writing a code in Android Python

To start with coding python on android, QPython3 is required, which can be downloaded from the internet.

Sample code:

```
Open Qpython3 and open an editor -
PYTHON:
Print "Hello world!!"
Save the file by extension .py
```

Implementation of Android Python using libraries

To use the library function in python, we just need to use the *"import"* statement and import a function from the *Python standard library.*

Ex:

```
from random import <package-name>
```

Python Scripting Layer

To create new applications using python, we need to access some real-time applications in a phone like a sensor, camera, etc... then a library called ***SL4A or Python android scripting layer*** can be used.

Here is a code to open the camera as well as saving the picture.

```
import sl4a
droid = sl4a.Android()
droid.cameraInteractiveCapturePicture("/sdcard/qpython_image
.jpg")
```

Code to Open a Web Page

```
from android import Android
droid = Android()
droid.webViewShow("https://www.google.com")
```

Python with Raspberry Pi

Raspberry PI is one of the most trending things which bought a computer to everyone's hand. This is a low-cost computing platform with which we can make computing available to everybody to learn to program.

Python is the most popular language and widely used in some modern applications, especially web applications and utilities.

Combination of Raspberry and Python

Python united with Raspberry pi can be used in many ways, as mentioned below:

- Can be used to learn how to program in python

- We can connect many numbers of sensors using raspberry pi and can receive and transmit data to the hardware systems

- If the program is written in python, the Raspberry can be used as a web server

- Designing many utilities using pi with code written in python can be used for monitoring and tracking purposes

- Both command line and IDE can be used to design

Python Packages

Python has many packages in it which can be used to perform many functionalities and packages needs to be installed in our local development environment

There are many packages available in Raspberry archives, and the best and most used way to install packages is to use *apt-get* methods.

Example:

```
sudo apt-get update
sudo apt-get install <python_package_name>
```

In case of requirement for any other package which is not available in Raspberry archives, we can use **standard Python Pip package management system.**

- The command used to install package from **Python Pip package management system** is as mentioned below:

```
Ex: $ pip3 install requests
```

The command used to show the current version of the installed package then we can use the below command;

```
Ex: $ pip3 show requests
Name: requests
Version: 2.4.5
Location: /user/lib/Python3/dist_packges
```

Python with Visual Studio

Visual Studio is a very powerful IDE on windows. Visual Studio enables open-source support for python language thorough data science.

Currently, Python is not available in visual studio for Mac, but it is available on Mac and Linux through visual studio code. Visual Studio supports multiple interpreters.

Features of Visual Studio with Python

- Editing and code comprehension:

Visual studio provides a Python editor which has auto coloring of syntax, formatting the code, signature, and refactoring, etc.

- Interactive window:

It has a feature like a python editor that can be directly opened within a visual studio rather than using a separate command prompt. Strong integration will be available between the python code editor and interactive window

CTRL+ENTER is used to step through the code without the use of a debugger.

- De-bugging:

Visual studio has python/C++ mixed mode debugging, remote debugging on LINUX, AZURE, and debugging within interactive windows.

Various unit testing tools will also be present in Visual studio

- Implementation of Azure SDK and Azure for Python

- Visual Studio enables CPython based interpreters and provides the ability of performance comparison among different profiling runs

Closure, Decorators, and Magic Functions

Python, as a language, provides us some great features to optimize our code and make it more readable. This document is about how we can significantly reduce the number of lines of code in Python using some advanced concepts.

What is Closure?

Let us take a look at the following piece of code.

```
def outer_function(y):
    x = 7
    def inner_add():
        return x + y
    return inner_add()


print(outer_function(3))
```

This code gives us the following output:

```
10
```

The *inner_add* function adds the number passed to *outer_function* as an argument with *x* and then returns the result to be printed.

We can see that the *inner_add* function is able to reference the value of *x,* which is defined outside the scope of the *inner_add* function itself. This is because of the "LEGB" rule for scopes in Python.

It is the order in which python looks for values and references within scopes.

L – *Local*

E – *Enclosing*

G – *Global*

B – *Built-in*

In our example, the value of *x* was found in the enclosing scope. So the *inner_add* function was able to reference it.

Also, we can see that the local function *inner_add* is returned from its defining scope and executed in another scope – the *print (outer_function (3))* statement. But, once a local function is returned from an enclosing scope, that enclosing scope is gone along with any local objects it defined.

So, how does the local function use bindings to the object (here it is the variable *x*) defined in a scope that no longer exists?

It is possible because the local function remembers the objects from the enclosing scope that it needs and prevents it from being garbage collected. This is called closure. ***Closures maintain references to objects from earlier scopes.***

Closures are best implemented in factory functions.

Factory Functions
Factory Functions take Variable(s) as Input and Return New, Specialized Functions.

In essence, the factory function has local functions inside it that return the specialized functions. The factory function takes some arguments, and the local function takes these arguments along with its own arguments to create a new function.

```
def multiply(times):
    def func(x):
        return "The answer is {}".format(x * times)
    return func


double = multiply(2)
triple = multiply(3)
print(double(4))
print(triple(4))
```

The output is:

```
The answer is 8
The answer is 12
```

As we can see, *multiply* is a factory function. It generated the functions *double* and *triple*.

```
double = multiply(2)
```

This bit of code calls the *multiply* function.

```
def func(x):
    return "The answer is {}".format(x*times)
return func
```

The control then comes to this part of the *multiply* function.

"func(x)" is a function that accepts an argument *"x"* and its job is to multiply *"x"* with the argument passed to the *multiply* function *("times")*. Then, it returns the instance of the *"func"* function.

From our code, we can see that *"double"* will hold a function that multiplies any number passed to it by two. A similar thing happens with *"triple."*

Also, since we are referencing *"times"* from inside *"func,"* we can see how closures are an integral part of factory functions.

Decorators

At a high level, decorators modify or enhance functions without changing their definitions. So, in essence, decorators are a lot like factory functions since they take functions as arguments and return functions. The difference being that the returned function is not a new function – it is the same function that was passed to the decorator, but it is modified or worked-on a bit. A decorator, in simple terms, is a function returning another function.

Decorator is any callable Python object which accepts the function being decorated as an argument, and the return value modifies the actual definition of the function. Similar to modifying a function, the decorator can also modify a method or class definition. But the decorator concept is less commonly used in classes.

When we want to decorate a function using a decorator, we write "@" followed by the name of the decorator function on top of the function to be decorated. Python itself has some in-built decorators like **classmethod ()** and **staticmethod ()**.

Python decorators share some similarities with Java annotations, and they have a similar syntax; the decorator syntax is simply a function transformation, using @ as the keyword:

Syntax

```
@decorator_function
def function():
    print("Hello")
```

Decorators aid in achieving metaprogramming as they enhance the behavior of the function/method they decorate.

Need for Decorators

1. Code duplication is a major concern as the programs get larger in the current software environment. Though simple code duplication is easier to tackle by dividing

into functions/methods, we need to find ways to tackle more complex duplications.

2. Another related issue is scattering of knowledge. For instance, suppose you need to locate all the functions with a common characteristic. We have the option of putting it in a separate external configuration file, but then there is a risk of the configuration file being out of sync. Whenever you add a new method or rename anything, you need to make sure it is added in the configuration file also which is double the typing.

So whatever be the case, duplication is a nightmare affecting both productivity and software reliability.

Decorators help in addressing both kinds of duplication. Decorators are callable Python objects which act as a wrapper around a function/method.

Uses of Decorators

Decorators can be termed as a variant of the design pattern named decorators, or rather its pythonic version. But there is very limited use of that. Python decorators can better be compared to macros.

- Decorators can be used for extending the behavior of an external lib to a function or for debugging purposes (when there is no need to make a temporary modification). Thereby you can extend the same behavior to several functions without rewriting it every time.

- Python decorators add extra functionality to another function

```
# A decorator is a function that accepts ANOTHER function as parameter
 def decorator_newone(fn_2_dec):
def wrapper_4_function():
        # The code to be executed BEFORE the original function
print "Before the function"
            # function call
fn_2_dec()
# The code to be executed AFTER the original function
print "After the function"
return wrapper_4_function

@decorator_newone
def another_function():
    print "Here comes the inner function"

another_function()
#outputs:
#Before the function
# Here comes the inner function
#After the function
```

Example 3: Adding extra functionality to a dummy function using decorator

Here the decorator is merely a shortcut for:

```
another_function = decorator_newone(another_function)
```

Decorators are usually wrappers, which lets you execute a piece of code before and after the function being decorated (without modifying the actual function).

Suppose there is a need to do certain logical activities at the entry and exit points of a function. It can be addressed using decorators, as shown below:

```
@entry
def function1():
    print "In function1()"

@entry
def function2():
    print "In function2()"

@new_Decorator
def randomFunction():
    print "In randomFunction"
```

Example 4: decorator at entry and exit – syntax

When the compiler parses this chunk of code, randomFunction() is compiled and the output object is sent to the new_Decorator code, which somehow creates a function-like object that to be substituted for the initial randomFunction().

```
class new_Decorator(object):
    def __init__(self, f):
        print "In new_Decorator.__init__()"
    def __call__(self):
        print "In new_Decorator.__call__()"


@new_Decorator
def randomFunction():
    print "In randomFunction()"


print "Done with decorator for randomFunction()"
randomFunction()
```

Example 5: decorator at entry and exit - sample

Upon running this code, the output is as below:

```
In new_Decorator.__init__()
In randomFunction()
Done with decorator for randomFunction ()
In new_Decorator.__call__()
```

Here, as you see, the constructor for new_Decorator is called while the decoration of the function is carried out.

The constructor receives the function object that is being decorated. Ideally, what happens is, the function object is fetched in the constructor and used later in the __call__() method.

When randomFunction() is decorated and then called the new_Decorator.__call__(), the method gets called instead of the actual code , i.e., it *replaces* the original function object with the resultant output of the decoration.

A simple chunk of code to depict how decorator aids in writing the same logic much more elegantly:

```
def do_nothing(): pass
do nothing = staticmethod(do_nothing)
 replaced by
@staticmethod
def do_nothing(): pass
```

Take a look at the below code:

```
def decorator(func):
    def wrapTheFunction():
        print("Before the func() call")
        func()
        print("After the func() call")
    return wrapTheFunction


@decorator
def a_function_requiring_decoration():
    print("Decorating")


a_function_requiring_decoration()
```

Output:

```
Before func() call
Decorating
After func() call
```

As the names suggest, *"decorator"* is the decorator function, and *"a_function_requiring_decoration"* is the function that we want to decorate.

But how does this work?

Whenever we invoke a decorator on a function, the compiler compiles the underlying function, but does not execute it. So, *"a_function_requiring_decoration"* is compiled first and then it is passed as an argument to the *"decorator"* function. The variable *"func"* will now store the function *"a_function_requiring_decoration"*. Now, the following block of code is executed.

def decorator(func):

```
    def wrapTheFunction():
        print("Before the func() call")
        func()
        print("After the func() call")
    return wrapTheFunction
```

This is what gives us our output:

```
Before func() call
Decorating
After func() call
```

"*wrapTheFunction*" is the function that is returned by the decorator and is mapped to "*a_function_requiring_decoration.*"

To simplify how the *decorator* function works, we can see the following line of code:

a_fucntion_requiring_decoration=decorator(a_function_req uiring_decoration)

Now, we have understood how decorators work. But there is still one problem with our code.

Using functools.wraps() method:

```
def decorator(func):
    def wrapTheFunction():
        print("Before the func() call")
        func()
        print("After the func() call")
    return wrapTheFunction

@decorator
def a_function_requiring_decoration():
    print("Decorating")
```

```
a_function_requiring_decoration()
print(a_function_requiring_decoration.__name__)
```

Output:

```
Before func() call
Decorating
After func() call
wrapTheFunction
```

We can see, that the call to the **__name__** attribute of *"a_function_requiring_decoration"* gives us the name *"wrapTheFunction"* when it should have been *"a_function_requiring_decoration"*. But how is that possible?

This is happening because we are returning *"wrapTheFunction"* from *"decorator,"* and it is replacing our function, overriding its name at the same time.

This can be easily solved by the *functools.wraps()* function provided by Python.

```
from functools import wraps
def decorator(func):
    @wraps
    def wrapTheFunction():
        print("Before the func() call")
        func()
        print("After the func() call")
    return wrapTheFunction

@decorator
def a_function_requiring_decoration():
```

```
    print("Decorating")

a_function_requiring_decoration()
print(a_function_requiring_decoration.__name__)
```

Output:

```
Before func() call
Decorating
After func() call
a_function_requiring_decoration
```

By using the *"@wraps()"* decorator on *wrapTheFunction*, we are allowing Python to pass the name from the previous decorator.

Chaining Decorators or Multiple Decorators

We can have multiple decorators decorating the same function. Let us take a look at how this happens:

```
from functools import wraps
def decorator1(func1):
    @wraps(func1)
    def wrapTheFunction1():
        print("Before the func1() call")
        func1()
        print("After the func1() call")
    return wrapTheFunction1

def decorator2(func2):
    @wraps(func2)
    def wrapTheFunction2():
```

```
        print("Before the func2() call")
        func2()
        print("After the func2() call")
    return wrapTheFunction2


@decorator1
@decorator2
def a_function_requiring_decoration():
    print("Decorating..")


a_function_requiring_decoration()
print(a_function_requiring_decoration.__name__)
```

Output:

```
Before the func1() call
Before the func2() call
Decorating..
After the func2() call
After the func1() call
a_function_requiring_decoration
```

This looks very different from what we might expect.

It seems as if the calls to *decorator1* and *decorator2* are interspersed with each other. That is exactly what happens when we have multiple decorators on a single function.

```
@decorator2
def a_function_requiring_decoration():
    print("Decorating..")
```

 The first decorator where control goes to is *decorator2*. But here, *decorator2* is decorated with *decorator1*.

```
@decorator1
@decorator2
def a_function_requiring_decoration():
    print("Decorating..")
```

So, *decorator1* takes *decorator2* as an argument and *decorator2* in turn takes *"a_function_requiring_decoration"* as its argument. This can be easily understood if we take *func1* as *decorator2* and *func2* as *"a_function_requiring_decoration"*.

```
def decorator1(func1):
    @wraps(func1)
    def wrapTheFunction1():
        print("Before the func1() call")
        func1()
        print("After the func1() call")
    return wrapTheFunction1

def decorator2(func2):
    @wraps(func2)
    def wrapTheFunction2():
        print("Before the func2() call")
        func2()
        print("After the func2() call")
    return wrapTheFunction2
```

When *decorator1* starts executing, we get the following:

Before the func1() call

Then *func1* is called, and control goes to *decorator2*. The output now becomes:

```
Before the func1() call
```

161

```
Before the func2() call
```

Next, when *func2* is called, control goes to *"a_function_requiring_decoration."*

Our output now is:

```
Before the func1() call
Before the func2() call
```

Decorating.

The control then flows back, and thus our final output is:

```
Before the func1() call
Before the func2() call
```

Decorating.

```
After the func2() call
After the func1() call
a_function_requiring_decoration
```

Stacking Two or More Decorators

When there is more than one decorator, we need to make sure that it is arranged in a compatible manner so that the maximum output is achieved.

The ordering of the decorators impacts the structure of the result. Thus, randomMethod is a class method descriptor wrapping a tracked instance wrapping the original randomMethod function. So, inner decorators are listed after outer decorators.

The basic thing to take care while we have multiple decorators is that you must know what kind of object each decorator takes as an argument and what it returns so that they can be arranged in a suitable wrapping order. The final idea is to make sure that the output of the inner decorator is compatible with the input of the immediate-outer decorator.

The built in decorators in Python namely *classmethod, staticmethod, and property* – each of them return attribute descriptors, hence their output cannot be passed to a decorator that expects a function. *classmethod* is put first in the below example for this reason.

class tracked:

```
    def __init__(self,fn):
        self.fn = fn
    def __call__(__self,*__args,**__kw):
        print "Entry to", __self.fn
        try:
            return __self.fn(*__args,**__kw)
        finally:
            print "Exit from", __self.fn
@tracked
def helloWorld():
    print "Hello WORLD!"
helloWorld()

class RandomClass(object):
    @classmethod
    @tracked
    def randomMethod(cls):
```

```
        print "Fetched within the class", cls
RandomClass.randomMethod()

class RandomClass(object):
    @classmethod
    @tracked
    def randomMethod(cls):
        print "Fetched within the class", cls
RandomClass.randomMethod()
```

Example 6: Arranging decorators for maximum output

Precautions while using Decorators

- Keep in mind that decorators are new as of Python 2.4, hence be sure to run your code on a compatible version.

- Once a function is decorated, it's done for all the code, you cannot undo it.

- The function call can slow down by the use of decorators. Hence use minimally.

- Decorators generally make your functions hard to debug as they wrap your functions.

But there is a solution available in Python 2.5 for the last issue. It provides the functools module, which includes functools.wraps (a decorator itself). It copies your function's name, module and docstring into its wrapper.

Magic Functions Overloading In Python

By defining certain methods by certain names, certain operations (for example, binary operations, arithmetic operations, etc.) can be implemented by a class in python by using certain syntax. That is how python allows classes to define their own behavior. This is called ***OPERATOR OVERLOADING*** *in python.*

"__" methods are also called magic methods. They are always surrounded by double underscores (e.g. __**init**__() or __**lt**__()).

Below is an example:

```
>>> class new_class:
    weight = 0
    def __init__(self, weight):
        self.weight = int(weight)
    def __add__(self, other):
        m1 = mango(self.weight)
        m1.weight = m1.weight + other.weight
        return m1

>>> def main():
        x = mango(5)
        y = mango(10)
        z = x + y
        print(z.weight)

>>> if __name__ == "__main__":
        main()
```

15

165

Overwriting the Operators

The operators can also be customized, allowing the class to define their own behavior. Examples of some key operator are given below.

"<" (__lt__()) and ">" (__gt__())

```
>>> class mango:
    weight = 0
    def __init__(self, weight):
        self.weight = int(weight)
    def __lt__(self, other):
        return self.weight.__lt__(other.weight)
    def __gt__(self,other):
        return self.weight.__gt__(other.weight)

>>> def main():
        a = mango(5)
        b = mango(10)
        print(a < b)
        print (a > b)

>>> if __name__ == "__main__":
        main()


True
False
```

"len()" (__len__())

```
>>> class fruit:
    def __init__(self, name):
        self.name = name
    def __len__(self):
```

```
        return len(self.name)

>>> def main():
        a = fruit("mango")
        print(len(a))

>>> if __name__ == "__main__":
        main()
```

5

"bool()" (__bool__())

```
>>> class fruit:
        b = True
        def __init__(self, inp):
            self.inp = inp
        def __bool__(self):
            m1 = fruit(self.inp)
            m1.b = bool(m1.inp)
            return m1.b


>>> def main():
        a = []
        b = ()
        c = [1]
        x = fruit(a)
        y = fruit(b)
        z = fruit(c)
        print(bool(a))
        print(bool(b))
        print(bool(c))
```

```
>>> if __name__ == "__main__":
        main()


False
False
True
```

"abs()" (__abs__())

```
>>> class fruit:
        def __init__(self, inp):
                self.inp = inp
        def __abs__(self):
                m1 = fruit(self.inp)
                return (abs(m1.inp))

>>> def main():
        x = 1000
        y = 8984
        a = fruit(x - y)
        b = abs(a)
        print(b)

>>> if __name__ == "__main__":
        main()


7984
```

"str()"

```
>>> class newClass:
        def __init__(self):
                pass

>>> def main():
```

```python
from datetime import datetime
now = datetime.now()
a = str(now)
b = str(newClass)
print (a+ " | "+b)
for r in a:
        print (r)
```

```
>>> >>> if __name__ == "__main__":
    main()
```

```
2015-02-21 16:28:18.133332 | <class '__main__.newClass'>
<
c
l
a
s
s

'
_
_
m
a
i
n
_
_
.
n
e
w
c
l
```

a

s

s

'

>

"next()"

```
>>> def main():
        x = ''
        g = 0
        m = [[1, 2, 3],[4, 5, 6],[7, 8, 9]]
        x = (sum(r) for r in m)
        y=
("("+str(row[2])+";"+str(row[1])+";"+str(row[0])+")" for row
in M)
        for i in m:
            print (next(x))
        for i in m:
            print (next(y))

>>> if __name__ == "__main__":
        main()
6
15
24
(3;2;1)
(6;5;4)
(9;8;7)
```

"eval()"

```
>>> from math import *
>>> def main():
        user_func = input("type a function: y = ")
        for x in range(1, 10):
            print ("x = ", x , ", y = ", eval(user_func))

>>> if __name__ == "__main__":
        main()
```

type a function: y = x**x

```
x = 1, y = 1
x = 2, y = 4
x = 3, y = 27
x = 4, y = 256
x = 5, y = 3125
x = 6, y = 46656
x = 7, y = 823543
x = 8, y = 16777216
x = 9, y = 387420489
```

Doctest for Python

Testing your Code

Writing the testing code and in parallel, running the code, is considered a good practice. This method helps in defining your code's intent more precisely and also having a decoupled architecture.

Some rules for testing:

1. A unit test should check each functionality for its correctness.

2. All the test units must be fully independent so that they can run regardless of the order in which they are called.

3. Try to make tests that run fast. Avoid using complex data structures to work as they may reduce the speed and in turn, will slow down the development.

4. Before writing any code, run a complete test suite, and run test suite again after coding is done.

5. It's good to make a hook, which will run all the test cases before code could be added to a shared repository.

6. If there is an interrupt in the middle of coding, then it is good to write broken test cases which help you to get the pointer where you left.

Modules for Python Testing

Python comes with many modules/libraries which can be used to test the Python code. Following are some of the modules that are generally used for testing:

Unittest

As 'JUnit' is a unit testing framework for Java, similarly python unit testing framework is sometimes referred to as 'PyUnit.'

Unittest provides test automation, shares setup and shutdown code for tests, aggregates test into a collection, and make tests that are independent of reporting framework. The unittest module provides inbuilt classes which use these qualities to write a set of tests.

Doctest

Test python code by running the documentation given in the program and verifying the result as expected. It parses the text in a document, finds examples, executes them, and then compares the output text with the expected value. It is easier than other python testing tools because there is no API to learn before using it and also there is no need to write separate test methods /functions. Just Doctest module needs to be imported. It searches the pieces of text inside code, which are similar to interactive Python session and then test these sessions.

Now we will see in detail how the Doctest module is used for testing the Python code.

Common ways of using Doctest are:

1. Write the docstring in module for all methods and check; all methods work as documented.

2. Write interactive examples in test files for a module or a complete package and verifying it by performing regression testing.

Using Docstring in Module for Testing

Docstring is any commented string which gives the documentation about the method or class. But while writing the docstring, which is used for testing that method or class, then it must be perfectly formatted.

Let us take one example to test two methods, 'division' and 'addition,' and writing a docstring for them.

For example:

```
"""
This is a docstring
>>> addition(10, 5)
15
>>> division(10, 2)
5
"""
def  addition(a, b):
        return a + b

def division(a.b):
        return a/b

if __name__ == "__main__":
    import doctest
    doctest.testmod( )
```

Now save the above example with example.py and run it. The program executes with no message, indicating that all the test cases are passed.

Now change the output in docstring as

```
>>> addition(10, 5)
10
```

Save the module and again execute it. The program executes with error message as below indicating the failure of test cases.

```
****************************************************************
File "__main__", line 9, in __main__
Failed example:
    addition(10, 5)
Expected:
    10
Got:
    15
****************************************************************
1 items had failures:
   1 of   2 in __main__
***Test Failed*** 1 failures.
```

If a user wishes to see the message for the success of test cases, then you need to run the module from the command prompt as:

```
>python example.py -v
```

Then it gives the output as

```
Trying:
    division(10, 2)
Expecting:
    5
ok
Trying:
    addition(10, 5)
Expecting:
    15
ok

1 items passed all tests:
2 tests in __main__
2 tests in 3 items.
```

```
2 passed and 0 failed.
Test passed.
```

Passing -v to the script prints a detailed log of what it's trying, and prints a summary at the end.

Using Docstring in a Text File for Testing

This is more beneficial than earlier method of using docstring because as the size of docstring becomes too large, it starts affecting the clarity of code, which is under testing. Also, it increases the reusability of code, as now the same test cases can be used for testing other code also.

Let us take one example to test two methods 'addition' and 'division,' which we have saved in example.py module. Delete the docstring from example.py module and save it.

For example

Create a text file with any name. Let us take example.txt and write the below docstring and save it.

```
>>> import python_doctest
>>> python_doctest.addition(10, 5)
15
>>> python_doctest.division(10, 2)
5
```

Now execute this text file by writing the following command in Python shell.

```
import doctest
doctest.testfile('example.txt')
```

This gives the output as

```
TestResults(failed = 0, attempted = 3)
```

Note: Free-floating text can also coexist with actual output. Also, it is not required to be placed in quotes. This helps in giving descriptions about the test scenarios.

Many useful examples can be found in test file Lib/test/test_doctest.py.

Points to Remember while using Doctest:

- Expected output must immediately follow the final '>>>' or '...' line with code.

- Expected output cannot contain only white spaces since it is treated as a signal for the end of the expected output.

- Output to stdout can only be captured. Output to stderr (Exception) is captured by different means.

- Doctest matches the output with exact value expected. Even if a single character doesn't match, then the test fails.

- Exact match also means that output must remain same on every run, so output you capture, you should not try to:

- Capture dictionary, because the order of items in it differs on every run.

- Capture floating-point numbers, as its precision, can vary across platforms.

Capture hard-coded address, such as <__main__.c>

How To Store And Authenticate Password In Python

Here are the basic steps on how to store and authenticate a password in Python.

Steps:

Refer to the attachment for a complete working solution.

We start by writing main script that will display a list of options to be selected by the end user.

```
import sys
import os
def main(argv):
    print ('\nPasswords Authentication Program v.01\n')
    print ('Please select one of below options:\n')
    print ('1. Store new user and password\n')
    print ('2. Authenticate user\n')
    print ('3. Exit program\n')
    user_input = input('Your selection (1/2/3): ')
    if user_input == "1":
        try:
            os.system("PasswordStorage.py
PasswordStorageFile.txt")
```

```
            except SystemExit:
                print ('PasswordStorage script stopped\n')
        elif user_input == "2":
            try:
                os.system("PasswordAuthentication.py
PasswordStorageFile.txt")
            except SystemExit:
                print ('PasswordAuthentication script
stopped\n')
        elif user_input == "3":
            sys.exit('Program Exited!')
        else:
            sys.exit('Program Exited!')
if __name__ == "__main__":
    main(sys.argv[1:])
```

This script will display the below-mentioned options to the user. This list will act as the main menu for the user:

1. Store new user and password

2. Authenticate user)

3. Exit program

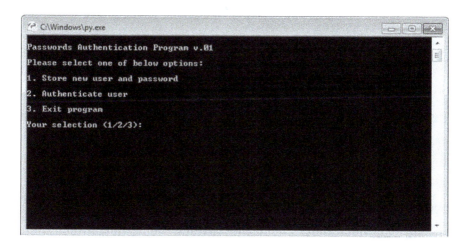

```
C:\Windows\py.exe                                          [ - ] [ □ ] [ X ]
Passwords Authentication Program v.01
Please select one of below options:
1. Store new user and password
2. Authenticate user
3. Exit program
Your selection (1/2/3):
```

1. Before authenticating a password, we need to figure out how to store a password. Below rules are followed to store a password:

   i. The password shouldn't be stored as plain text.

   ii. The password should confirm to below-mentioned policy:

      a. The length should be nine characters.

      b. It should contain one or more uppercase letters.

      c. It should contain one or more lowercase letters.

      d. It should contain one or more numbers.

      e. It should contain one or more special characters.

   iii. Password expiry policy should be implemented.

181

2. Script for storing passwords.

The script accepts username and password and stores it in a text file. Before saving the password, it checks whether the password satisfies the above said rules by using a regular expression: "(?=.{9,})(?=.*?[^\w\s])(?=.*?[0-9])(?=.*?[A-Z]).*?[a-z].*"

It also ensures that the password is not stored as plain text. The script uses the SHA224 algorithm to encrypt the password before saving. We have used Lib/hashlib.py library, which implements a common interface to many different secure hash and message digest algorithms. Here is how the stored user name and password will look like:

mary;dd7d3112e7006f0439b10e9f6e7ee29d8c159f837a55a6173 d8ed5a5;18/11/2019 18:53:06

The datetime of when the password is generated is also saved. It'll be used for a password expiry check.

After the script execution has completed, it returns back to the main menu.

3. Script for password authentication.

```
import sys
import hashlib
import getpass
import os
import datetime
def process_file(file_name):
```

```python
    user_names = []
    passwords = []
    date_time = []
    try:
        file_conn = open(file_name)
        data = file_conn.readlines()
        for i in range(len(data)):
            words = (data[i][:-1]).split(";")
            user_names.append(words[0])
            passwords.append(words[1])
            date_time.append(words[2])
        file_conn.close()
    except:
        sys.exit('There was a problem reading the file!')
    return user_names, passwords, date_time
def main(argv):
    if len(argv) != 1:
        sys.exit('Usage: PasswordAuthentication.py
<file_name>')
    print ('\nUser and Password Authentication Program
v.01\n')
    user_names, passwords, date_time =
process_file(sys.argv[1])
    pass_try = 0
    x = 3
    user = input('Please Enter User Name: ')
    user_found = 1
    if user not in user_names:
        print('Unkown User Name, returning to main menu...
\n')
        user_found = 0
    if user_found:
        while pass_try < x:
```

```python
            user_input =
hashlib.sha224(getpass.getpass('Please Enter Password:
').encode()).hexdigest()
            if user_input !=
passwords[user_names.index(user)]:
                pass_try += 1
                print ('Incorrect Password, ' + str(x-
pass_try) + ' more attemts left\n')
            else:
                pass_try = x+1
                present = datetime.datetime.now()
                password_creation_datetime =
date_time[user_names.index(user)]
                date_object =
datetime.datetime.strptime(password_creation_datetime,
'%d/%m/%Y %H:%M:%S')
                difference = present - date_object
                if difference >=
datetime.timedelta(30,0,0,0,0,0,0):
                    print ('Password has expired. It has to
be renewed every 30 days. Returning to main menu...\n')
                user_found = 0

    if pass_try == x:
        print('Incorrect Password, Returning to main menu...
\n')
    elif user_found:
        print ('User is logged in! Returning to main
menu...\n')
    os.system("AuthenticationModule.py")
if __name__ == "__main__":
    main(sys.argv[1:])
```

This script authenticates the passwords that are stored in the above-mentioned text file. Following functionalities have been implemented:

- The password is authenticated using the SHA224 algorithm.

- Only three attempts are given to enter the correct password

- Password will expire after 30 days

- If the user name is not found, then return to the main menu.

Specialized Container Datatypes in Python

Introduction

The container classes introduced in the older versions of python have been extended to provide a new set of specialized container data types which overcome the drawbacks and add extra features to help users develop applications with ease without having to bother about the internal implementations. This document explains when to use these specialized container data types and what advantages it gives over the conventional containers like a dictionary, list, and tuples.

The containers introduced after Python 2.7 are:

1. Ordered Dictionaries

2. Named Tuples

3. Default Dictionaries

4. ChainMaps

Ordered Dictionaries

The classic python dictionary, as we know consists of the key-value pairs.

Python dictionary is a hash table and doesn't preserve the order. And hence, the output could either be "key1 key2" or "key2 key1". This is the main drawback in using python dictionaries.

If the order of insertion is one of the desired features of the application you are developing, then OrderedDict introduced in Python 2.7 can be used. The ordered dictionary inherits from the dictionary class, and it preserves the order of insertion of keys into the dictionaries. Currently ordered dictionary is represented as a list of tuples instead of key: value notation. Rewriting the code with an ordered dictionary and checking the output will always give you "key1 key2" as it remembers the order in which the items are inserted.

On inserting an item for which the key already exists, the order doesn't get changed. In other words, a key's value can be changed without disturbing the order.

```
Ord_dict = collections.OrderedDict([])
Ord_dict[1] = "value1"
Ord_dict[2] = "value2"
Ord_dict[3] = "value3"
```

If we get list(Ord_dict(keys)) we get the list [1, 2, 3].Then we change the value of the 1st key with Ord_dict[1] = "value4" and again get the list of keys, the order of keys is unchanged.

To move an item to the end of the list, we must first remove it from the list and then re-insert it. To remove an item at the end of the list(LIFO, use popitem(). To remove an item in FIFO order, use popitem(last = false), which returns the first item in the list.

Another use of using ordered dictionaries is for sorting. In the application, you are designing if there is a need to iterate through the dictionary multiple times, then sorting the dict makes it efficient. The items will be deleted in order, but inserting would append it at the end of the list and does not preserve the sort order.

```
collections.OrderedDict(sorted(dict.items()))
```

Default Dictionaries

When accessing a normal python dictionary, if we happen to use a key that's not part of the dictionary, then we get a "keyError." There may be a case in our application that we do not want to get the error, instead, if the key doesn't exist, we want to add the entry and return the newly created item's value. In such a scenario, we can use the default dictionary. The factory function gets called when the key is not present.

```
Collections.defaultdict(default_factory)
```

When we fetch the items of the dictionary, we get the default value for the items for which the key doesn't exist.

```
>>> defaultDict.items()
[('key2', 'x'), ('key1', 'val1')]
>>>
```

Named Tuples

Simple data structures can be represented using Tuples. For example to represent a network address

```
NetAdd = (hostname, port)
```

To access the individual elements we have to use index positions NetAdd[0] and NetAdd[1]. This makes the code hard to read and maintain.

To overcome this problem, we can use named tuples using which we can refer to items with both names and index positions. This becomes very useful when dealing with large amounts of data where you want to fetch a field by its name and not its index position.

```
namedtuple(typename, field_names[, verbose = False][, rename
= False])
```

The benefit of using named tuple is that it is memory efficient, and there are many built-in functions to help the program easily.

If you are designing your application with many functions returning multiple values, then it is efficient to use named tuples over dictionaries and conventional tuples as you don't have the overhead to populate and maintain a whole dictionary, however, we need to take into consideration that named tuples are immutable.

ChainMaps

Python 3.3 introduces a new container class called the chainMaps.

When there is a need to perform a lookup operation on multiple dictionaries, maybe to find the existence of a particular key, ChainMaps can be used. It eases the process by logically merging the dictionaries into a single mapping to perform specific operations. Remember that these mappings are not merged; instead, ChainMap keeps a list of these dictionaries and redefines common dictionary operations to scan the list.

Example:

```
from collections import ChainMap
Dict1 = {'a': 1, 'b':2}
Dict2 = {'c': 3, 'b':4}
CMap = ChainMap(Dict1, Dict2)
Print(CMap['a'])
Print(CMap['b'])
Print(CMap['c'])
```

We can use the common dictionary operation on this ChainMaps

```
Len(CMap)
List(CMap.keys())
```

```
List (CMap .values())
```

ChainMaps can be substituted for update dictionaries also which will merge multiple dictionaries.

But there is an overhead of creating a separate dictionary. And most importantly, if the original dictionary is modified, the changes do not reflect in the merged dictionary.

Performance Evaluation of
Data Structures in Python

Introduction

Python is a pure object-oriented scripting language. Python implements simple syntax and a highly coherent programming model. Python is known for the speed of development because of simple syntax and no steps for compilation. Python also had built-in toolset helping the developers in fast programming. Python programs run on most computer platforms. Python has a large collection of the standard library. Jython and Iron Python are available as Java-based and .net- based versions of Python, respectively. In this document, the performance of various data structures in searching for a given key value in the database is compared.

Mega applications like Facebook make use of multiple technology components to deal with all the complexities associated with their size. In deciding a technology for an upcoming software component, architects are finding it difficult to make decisions on the choice of technology. Taking cognizance of the fact that most of the performance-based challenges involve searching vast data stores, the document deals with finding the response of Python technology to search operations using data structures. And also, Python is used mostly in huge data-centric and precision centric applications like Health care, finance, biometrics, etc.

Comparative Study of Speeds of Various Data Structures in Python for Locating a Key Value in Search Operations

In this chapter, we study the time taken by different data structures for searching the same key value at different positions in the database. The data structures taken for the study are:

1. Linked List

2. Queue - First in First out (FIFO)

3. Binary Search Tree

4. Self-Balancing Binary Search Tree or Adelson-Velskii and Landis Tree (AVL Tree)

5. Red Black Tree

These data structures are created from a million records where the key-value being searched is of **type string**. These records are taken from an existing large database. Then pre-decided key values at fixed locations are searched for using the different data structures, and the speeds are being compared. The code created to study performance using the above-mentioned data structure would be that readily available as part of the language API, and in its absence, we would use custom code which is readily available in Python. The observations would involve searching four key values of the type String, namely those at the first, 500,001st, 1,000,000th position, and a nonexistent record.

Observation

The search operations were performed 100 times for each record, i.e. first record, middle record, last record, and a non-existing record, and graphs have been plotted with taking time as a median of all the time recorded. Below shown are the graphs and various inferences made using them for each of the data structures under study.

Linked List

Time taken to search various records in a Queue in Linked list

The first record took 0 nanoseconds.

The middle record took 1.39 nanoseconds.

The last record took 2.81 nanoseconds.

No record took 2.80 nanoseconds.

Queue

Time taken to search various records in a Queue in Python

The first record took 0 nanoseconds.

The middle record took 1.39 nanoseconds.

The last record took 2.81 nanoseconds.

No record took 2.78 nanoseconds.

Binary Tree

Time taken to search various records in a Binary Tree of Python:

The first record took 0 nanoseconds.

The middle record took 0 nanoseconds.

The last record took 0 nanoseconds.

No record took 0 nanoseconds.

AVL Tree

Time taken to search various records in an Avl Tree of Python:

The first record took 0 nanoseconds.

The middle record took 0 nanoseconds.

The last record took 0 nanoseconds.

No record took 0 nanoseconds.

Red-Black Tree

Time taken to search various records in a Red-Black Tree of Python:

The first record took 0 nanoseconds.

The middle record took 0 nanoseconds.

The last record took 0 nanoseconds.

No record took 0 nanoseconds.

Interesting Observation

Python observations showed some outlying points which appeared at random without any distinct pattern of occurrence and that too only for the Tree data structures.

The table below shows the time taken in nanoseconds by various data structures to search records at various positions as per the above observations, and correspondingly, a graph is plotted:

	First Record	Middle Record	Last Record	Nonexistent Record
Linked List	0	1.398000002	2.813299966	2.804399991
Queue	0	1.393099976	2.814599967	2.784200025
Binary Tree	0	0	0	0
AVL Tree	0	0	0	0
RB Tree	0	0	0	0

From the above details, it is clear that Tree data structures take the least time for searching any record whereas the search operation is done in Linked Lists, and Queue data structures take a similar curve without much deviation from each other.

Reference Code

Here is a code written for a linked list.

```
import time
import MySQLdb

class Link:
    nextLink = None
    def __init__(self, name):
        self.nameFind = name
```

```python
    def showCurrentLink(self):
        print self.nameFind


class LinkList:
    firstLink  = Link(None)
    def empty(self):
        if(self.firstLink == None):
            return True
        else:
            return False


    def addLink(self, name):
        link1 = Link(name)
        link1.nextLink = self.firstLink
        self.firstLink = link1
        return self.firstLink


    def deleteLink(self):
        latest = Link(self.firstLink)
        self.firstLink = self.firstLink.nextLink
        return latest


    def displayLinkList(self):
        print "LinkList in descending order :\n"
        counter = self.firstLink
        while (counter != None):
            counter.showCurrentLink()
            counter = counter.nextLink


    def  find(self,key):
        counter = self.firstLink
        while(counter.nameFind != key):
            if(counter.nextLink == None):
                return None
```

```
            else:
                counter = counter.nextLink; # go to next
link
        return counter; # found it


l1 = LinkList()
# First we will be opening the database connection
db1 = MySQLdb.connect("localhost","root","root","myDB" )

# Now we will be preparing a cursor object with the help of
cursor() method
cursor = db1.cursor()

# Now, we will use the SQL query for reading every record
present in the database.
sqlstatement = "SELECT * FROM datatable"

try:
    cursor.execute(sqlstatement)
    finalresults = cursor.fetchall()
    for allrow in finalresults:
        l1.addLink(allrow[1])
except:
    print "No data found or unable to fetch."

# disconnect from server
db.close()

# l1.displayLinkList()

start = time.time()

l1.find("mary")
```

```python
total = time.time() - start

print "Time taken = %10.9f" % total

resultFind = Link(None)

resultFind = ll.find("mary")

if(resultFind != None):
    print resultFind.nameFind
else:
    print "Sorry value asked is not in our database\n"
```

Conclusion

Now since you have learned the tips and tricks in Python for writing better code, you will be able to optimize your code and make its execution time faster than it was before. The performance tuning tips for Python will not only help you in making your code fast but will also use fewer system resources and memory space. This is very crucial in today's modern world of programming as the focus has shifted from writing codes to writing best performing codes. By following the best coding standards while writing your Python code will make your code more readable and reusable for other developers. Then the need for Magic functions in Python has arisen in the recent past, and it helps in operator overloading. The specialized container datatypes have helped you in understanding ordered dictionaries, default dictionaries, named tuples, and ChainMaps.

We also evaluated the performance of various data structures in Python and recorded their observations. It is very helpful in deciding which data structure to use for sorting and which one will give the desired results. Apart from this, the emphasis was made on Doctest for Python, to make you understand how the Python code is tested, modules used for testing, what points should be taken care of while using doctest, and how to store passwords in python. I hope you liked the book, and it will help you in learning the tips and tricks for writing better codes in Python.

References

www.python.org

http://docs.python.org/3/library/profile.html

http://pypy.org/performance.html

https://wiki.python.org/moin/PythonSpeed/PerformanceTips

Head First Python, Paul Barry, 2011

www.ingramcontent.com/pod-product-compliance
Lightning Source LLC
Chambersburg PA
CBHW071116050326
40690CB00008B/1239